SUPPLE

M000031493

THE EVERYDAY WRITER

Fifth Edition

Lex Runciman
LINFIELD COLLEGE

Carolyn Lengel

Kate Silverstein

BEDFORD/ST. MARTIN'S
BOSTON ✦ NEW YORK

For information, write: Bedford/St. Martin's, 75 Arlington Street, Boston, MA 02116   (617-399-4000)

ISBN: 978-1-4576-2251-9

Preface

Supplemental Exercises for The Everyday Writer is a resource for teachers and students. Its exercises consist of sentences and paragraphs needing revision, most of them designed so that students can edit directly on the pages of this book.

The exercise sets are numbered to correspond to chapters in *The Everyday Writer,* so that students can quickly locate help by following the cross-references in each exercise's instructions.

To help students check their own progress as they work, answers to the even-numbered exercise items appear in the back of this book. Exercises with many possible answers — those asking students to imitate a sentence or revise a paragraph, for example — are not answered here. Answers to the odd-numbered exercises are given in the instructor's answer key only, which is available for download on the book's Web site.

If you have adopted *The Everyday Writer* as a text, you are welcome to photocopy any of these exercises to use for homework assignments, for classroom activities, or for quizzes. The book is also available for student purchase. Also available on our Web site are additional exercises for practice: **bedfordstmartins.com/everydaywriter**.

Contents

PUNCTUATION AND MECHANICS   92

FOR MULTILINGUAL WRITERS   121

ANSWERS TO THE EVEN-NUMBERED EXERCISES   134

Writing for College and Beyond

1.1 The top twenty: A quick guide to troubleshooting your writing

The following sentences are drawn from a researched argument using two sources: "Because Partying Is Too Mainstream: Alternative Spring Breaks" by Valeria Delgado (Collegemagazine.com, March 20, 2012) and "We Did Not Give Up Our Spring Break, We Took Advantage of It" from a United Way blog post (Unitedway.org, March 11, 2012). Revise each numbered item to eliminate one of the twenty most common sentence-level errors written by first-year students. (See *The Everyday Writer*, Chapter 1.) Example:

> **College students are usually eager to spend S̶p̶r̶i̶n̶g̶ _spring_ break having as much fun as possible.**

1. After months of stressful schoolwork, students understandably want to spend the week relaxing or blowing off steam with there friends.

2. Popular spring break destinies over the years have included Mexican resorts, Florida beaches, and Caribbean islands.

3. A growing number of students, however, are beginning to recognize that its actually rewarding to spend vacation time in more useful ways.

4. A new trend, known as alternative spring breaks, allows college students to contribute their time to humanitarian causes. Or environmental organizations.

5. Each year, thousands of students decide to skip the wild party scenes, they choose instead to do something meaningful for people or places in need.

6. There are a host of options available to students who want to volunteer over their spring break. "Programs range from working with kids in U.S. cities to building sustainable water systems in Nicaragua" (Delgado).

7. Usually a student will seek out a volunteer opportunity that best suits their talents and interests. Of course, many students still want to go somewhere warm.

8. Students can find the best match for their interests and desired location with the help of large nonprofit organizations such as United Way. They also frequently subsidize the costs of the trips to make them more affordable.

9. Although volunteering opportunities have always been available to students, the concept of alternative spring breaks is fairly recent. United Way began setting alternative spring breaks in 2006.

10. Some students work within their own communities others may travel thousands of miles to volunteer over spring break.

11. Services that students provide include, painting community centers, planting trees in parks, cleaning up the environment, and teaching English as a second language.

12. In Michigan, students who renovated a community recreation center and added a reading corner to encourage children to read after school each day.

13. In New Orleans, Habitat for Humanity has brought students together to help build new-houses for people who lost their homes in Hurricane Katrina in 2005.

14. On the Gulf Coast where the 2010 oil spill devastated shorelines students have helped clean up beaches and safeguard sea turtle nests.

15. Some students have traveled to Rock Hill, south Carolina, to clean up an old cemetery and repair homes on the Catawba Indian Reservation.

16. All students have their own reasons for embarking on an alternative spring break but many find that they come away with benefits they had not anticipated.

17. According to one source, students may go on an alternative spring break to improve their résumé or to take an affordable trip, but they end up having an important emotional experience and building lifelong memories.

18. Moreover, as noted in a United Way blog entry, "What many students don't realize until they arrive is the impact it will have on their own lives". ("We Did Not Give Up")

19. According to Valeria Delgado, one student reluctantly volunteered at the Boys and Girls Club in Newark, New Jersey, over spring break in 2011 and finds that he enjoyed it much more than he thought he would ("Because Partying Is Too Mainstream").

20. Another student Delgado interviewed found that through helping others he was actually helping himself. After volunteering with poor families in south Mississippi he realized how fortunate he was and gained a better sense of his priorities in life ("Because Partying Is Too Mainstream").

Critical Thinking and Argument

13.1 Using the Toulmin system

Use the seven-part Toulmin system to begin to develop an argument for one of the following questions. Here is the Toulmin system:

1. Make your claim.
2. Restate or qualify your claim.
3. Present good reasons to support your claim.
4. Explain the underlying assumptions that connect your claim and your reasons. If an underlying assumption is controversial, provide backing for it.
5. Provide additional grounds to support your claim.
6. Acknowledge and respond to possible counterarguments.
7. Draw a conclusion, stated as strongly as possible.

(See *The Everyday Writer*, section 13d.)

1. Should the Pledge of Allegiance include the phrase "Under God," or should that phrase be omitted?

2. Should schools be responsible for children's moral education, or should a child's moral development be solely the concern of the parents?

13.2 Recognizing fallacies

Locate any fallacies in the sentences below. Identify the name of the particular fallacy (for example, "bandwagon appeal"). Then write out a sentence or two explaining your reasoning. If a sentence contains an effective argument, write *no fallacy*. (See *The Everyday Writer*, section 13e.) Example:

> **Instead of supporting the hunger initiative, that candidate believes that poor people should simply starve to death.**

Fallacy: _straw man_____

Explanation: _This sentence makes the highly unlikely claim that a_____

_candidate who disagrees with the author's view must therefore want_____

_people to starve._____

1. Addie almost made the Dean's list last semester, and this semester she has been studying even harder and getting better grades. Chances are good that she will make the Dean's list this time.

2. Successful, financially secure people have high credit scores. Find out how high your credit score is at getyourcreditreport.com.

3. A well-known Hollywood actress claims that this weight loss plan is safe and effective, so I'm going to give it a try.

4. Everyone is talking about the new series on HBO. Don't miss the next episode this Sunday night!

5. Last summer's temperatures were much cooler than average. Global warming is clearly not a reality.

6. You obviously understand the importance of saving for retirement, and gold is the safest investment you can make.

7. This restaurant is in a wonderful location with exceptional views, and the prices are very high; therefore, the food must be excellent.

8. If we legalized the sale of marijuana, drug problems in this country would disappear.

9. It is true that we need real tax reform in this country, but I refuse to listen to the ideas of a senator who cheats on his wife and refers to grown women as "girls."

10. If you don't attend an elite private high school, there is no way you will be accepted into an Ivy League college.

14.1 Recognizing arguable statements

The following sentences include either arguable statements of opinion or statements of fact. Sentences that include citation information are drawn from two sources: "Putting Meat on the Table: Industrial Farm Animal Production in America" by the Pew Commission on Industrial Farm Animal Production (http://www.ncifap.org/_images/PCIFAPFin .pdf, 2008) and "Flesh of Your Flesh: Should You Eat Meat?" by Elizabeth Kolbert (*New Yorker*, November 9, 2009). Indicate which of the following sentences are arguable and which are factual by filling in the blank after each sentence with *arguable* or *factual*. (See *The Everyday Writer*, section 14a.) Example:

> **One of the best health decisions a person can make is to become a**
>
> **vegetarian.** _arguable_

1. Humans were never intended to eat meat, and we would all live longer, healthier lives if we stopped eating it. _____

2. Health experts agree that vegetarians tend to have lower blood pressure and a lower mortality rate from heart disease than meat eaters do.

    _____

3. Moreover, killing animals for food is cruel, unethical, and unnecessary.

    _____

4. According to the Pew Commission on Industrial Farm Animal Production, the average American consumed 221 pounds of red meat in 2005 (3). _____

5. An article in the *New Yorker* points out that each year in this country, roughly 30 million cows, more than 115 million pigs, and as many as 9 billion birds are killed for food (Kolbert, 74). _____

6. During World War I, the U.S. government encouraged citizens to eat vegetarian diets one day per week—on "Meatless Tuesdays"—to conserve meat for the troops. _____

7. Upton Sinclair's 1906 book *The Jungle* exposed the dirty, unsafe, and exploitive working conditions in Chicago's meatpacking plants. _____

8. Nothing is more disgusting than the way animals in slaughterhouses are killed for their meat. _____

9. Obviously, meat eaters do not care as much about environmental problems and world hunger as vegetarians do. _____

10. Vegetarians can live with a clear conscience about their diets. _____

14.2 Demonstrating fairness

Study carefully the following advertisement for the United Way. Then briefly answer each of the following questions

1. How do the writers of this advertisement establish common ground?

2. How do they demonstrate fairness?

3. How do they shape their appeal?

(See *The Everyday Writer*, section 14e.)

Language

21.1 Identifying stereotypes

Each of the following sentences stereotypes a person or a group of people. Underline the word or phrase that identifies the stereotyped person or group. In each case, be ready to explain why the stereotype may be offensive, demeaning, or unfair. (See *The Everyday Writer,* section 21a.) Example:

> **If you have trouble printing, ask a <u>computer geek</u> for help.**
>
> Assumes that all computer-savvy people are geeky, which is not the case.

1. For a blue-collar worker, he was extremely well read.

2. All women just adore those flowery romance novels!

3. I wanted an Eastern European housekeeper, because everyone knows they are the most thorough cleaners.

4. Did you see a chiropractor or a real doctor for your back problem?

5. Everyone in the South prefers the Confederate flag to that of the United States.

6. I know that he shouldn't have made those lewd remarks to the girl on the school bus, but boys will be boys.

7. How wonderful that you are adopting a child! Were you unable to have children of your own?

8. Those third-graders were attentive, focused, and calm during the presentation. I guess they all took their Ritalin this morning.

9

21.2 Identifying and revising sexist language

The following excerpt is taken from a 1961 publication by the U.S. Department of Agriculture's Office of the General Counsel. Read it carefully, noting any language we might today consider sexist. Then try bringing the language up to date by revising the passage, substituting nonsexist language as necessary. (See *The Everyday Writer*, section 21b.)

Your Role as a Lawyer in the Department of Agriculture

A stimulating and rewarding career awaits you as a lawyer in the U.S. Department of Agriculture. You will be a member of a 200-man legal staff in the Office of the General Counsel, which performs all the legal work for the Department. You will find an opportunity to practice in the field of your interest. . . .

An attorney in the Office of the General Counsel has personal contact with the administrative officials who are his clients. He furnishes legal advice directly to these clients through all stages in the development, administration, and enforcement of departmental programs. The lawyer is not restricted to a narrow field of legal activity. He has an opportunity to engage in many legal functions that relate to his assigned program area. He gives oral advice, writes opinions and briefs, drafts all kinds of legal documents and regulations, drafts and interprets legislation, and engages in hearings and trial work.

Because of the volume and importance of the legal services that must be performed, an attorney in the Office of the General Counsel has an opportunity to handle complex and responsible legal work at an earlier stage in his career than in private practice. In addition, he is free from the personal and economic problems of individual clients.

21.3 Rewriting to eliminate offensive references

Review the following sentences for offensive references or terms. If a sentence seems acceptable as written, write C. If a sentence contains unacceptable terms, rewrite it. (See *The Everyday Writer*, Chapter 21.) Example:

Passengers
~~Elderly passengers~~ on the cruise ship *Romance Afloat* will enjoy
^
swimming, shuffleboard, and nightly movies.

1. The doctor and the male nurse had different manners when tending to the patients in their care.

2. All of the children in the kindergarten class will ask their mothers to help make cookies for the bake sale.

3. The Oriental girl who works at the bank is always pleasant and efficient.

4. Acting as a spokesman and speaking with a southern twang, Cynthia McDowell, attractive mother of two, vowed that all elementary school-teachers in the district would take their turns on the picket line until the school board agreed to resume negotiations.

5. If you get lost, just ask a policeman if he can assist you.

6. Seventy-six-year-old Jewish violinist Josh Mickle, last night's featured soloist, brought the crowd to its feet.

7. Our skylight was installed last week by a woman carpenter.

8. The interdenominational service was attended by Jews, Christians, Buddhists, and Arabs.

9. Blind psychology professor Dr. Charles Warnath gave the keynote address last night.

10. Catholic attorney Margaret Samuelson won her sixteenth case in a row last week.

22.1 Considering ethnic and regional varieties of English

Read the following examples by authors using ethnic and regional varieties of English. See if you can "translate" each of them into standard academic English. Once you have your translated sentences, write a brief paragraph (in standard academic English) discussing (1) the differences you detect between standard academic English and the ethnic or regional example, and (2) the effects that are achieved by using each variety of English. (See *The Everyday Writer*, sections 22b and c.)

Miss Glory and I were washing up the lunch dishes when Mrs. Cullinan came to the doorway. "Mary?". . .

Miss Glory's face was a wonder to see. "You mean Margaret, ma'am. Her name's Margaret."

"That's too long. She's Mary from now on.". . .

Miss Glory had a fleeting second of feeling sorry for me. Then as she handed me the hot tureen she said, "Don't mind, don't pay that no mind. Sticks and stones may break your bones, but words. . . . You know, I been working here for twenty years."

She held the back door open for me. "Twenty years. I wasn't much older than you. My name used to be Hallelujah. That's what Ma named me, but my mistress give me 'Glory,' and it stuck. I likes it better too."

–MAYA ANGELOU, *I Know Why the Caged Bird Sings*

"Why don't you like me the way I am? I'm *not* a genius! I can't play the piano. And even if I could, I wouldn't go on TV if you paid me a million dollars!" I cried.

My mother slapped me. "Who ask you be genius?" she shouted. "Only ask you be your best. For you sake. You think I want you be genius? Hnnh! What for! Who ask you!" – AMY TAN, *The Joy Luck Club*

23.1 Using appropriate formality

Revise each of the following sentences to use appropriate formality consistently, eliminating colloquial or slang terms. (See *The Everyday Writer*, section 23a.) Example:

> Although be excited   as soon as
> **I can ~~get all enthused~~ about writing, ~~but~~ I sit down to write my**
> ^   ^ blank.   ^
> **mind goes ~~right to sleep.~~**
>   ^

1. At the conclusion of Jane Austen's classic novel *Pride and Prejudice*, the two eldest Bennett sisters both get hitched.

2. I agree with many of his environmental policies, but that proposal is totally nuts.

3. The celebrated Shakespearean actor gave the performance of a lifetime, despite the lame supporting cast.

4. We decided not to buy a bigger car that got lousy gas mileage and instead to keep our old Honda.

5. Often, instead of firing an incompetent teacher, school officials will transfer the person to another school in order to avoid the hassles involved in a dismissal.

6. After she had raced to the post office at ten minutes to five, she realized that she had completely spaced the fact that it was a federal holiday.

7. Desdemona's attitude is that of a wimp; she just lies down and dies, accepting her death as inevitable.

8. Moby Dick's humongous size was matched only by Ahab's obsessive desire to wipe him out.

9. The refugees had suffered great hardships, but now they were able to see the light at the end of the tunnel.

10. The class misbehaved so dreadfully in their regular teacher's absence

    that the substitute lost it.

23.2 Determining levels of language

For each of the scenarios below, note who the audience would be for the piece of writing. Then circle the level of formality that would be appropriate. Be prepared to explain your answer. (See *The Everyday Writer,* section 23a.) Example:

> **An Internet chat room for people who are interested in Harley-**
>
> **Davidson motorcycles**
>
> **Level of formality:**
>
> (informal)   formal
>
> **Audience:** _____ *others who share your passion* _____

1. An email to a childhood friend across the country

    Level of formality:

    informal   formal

    Audience: _____

2. A letter requesting an interview in response to a help-wanted advertise-
    ment in the newspaper

    Level of formality:

    informal   formal

    Audience: _____

3. A brochure explaining the recycling policies of your community to local
    residents

    Level of formality:

    informal   formal

    Audience: _____

4. A letter to the editor of the *Washington Post* explaining that a recent editorial failed to consider all the facts about health maintenance organizations (HMOs)

   Level of formality:

   informal   formal

   Audience: _____

5. A cover letter asking a professor to accept the late paper you are sending after the end of the semester

   Level of formality:

   informal   formal

   Audience: _____

23.3 Checking for correct denotation

Read each of the following sentences, looking for errors in denotation and using your dictionary as needed. Cross out every error that you find. Then examine each error to determine the word intended, and write in the correct word. If a sentence has no error, write C. (See *The Everyday Writer*, section 23b.) Example:

> **Some schools are questioning whether selling bottled water on**
> decision
> **campus is the right ~~incision~~ for the environment.**
> ^

1. Even if recycling is avoidable on campus, many bottles end up in the trash, adding to landfill waste.

2. Some students abdicate the use of refillable plastic bottles, which they can fill up at home or at water stations on campus.

3. Other students think drinking fountains should suffice to keep the school population hydrogenated.

4. Some students favor the sale of bottled water on campus, and they think it is unfair to sell other items in vending machines while bottled water is exuded.

5. These students ascertain that they should be allowed to purchase water just like they can purchase soda or candy bars.

6. Administrators feel pressure not only from both sides of students, but also from their vendors.

7. For example, if they refuse to sell Dasani bottled water, they may lose their vending contract with Coca-Cola, and that could cost the schools money.

8. There may be a comprise solution that considers the concerns of all the different groups.

9. For starters, administrators could make certain that drinking fountains are kept clean and in working order.

10. In addition, bottled water sales could be limited, and recycling bins could be made more readily avoidable for all plastic bottles.

23.4   Revising sentences to change connotations

The sentences that follow contain words with strongly judgmental connotative meanings. Underline these words; then revise each sentence to make it more neutral. (See *The Everyday Writer*, section 23b.) Example:

> **The current NRA <u>scheme</u> appeals to patriotism as a <u>smokescreen to obscure the real issue</u> of gun control.**
>
> The current NRA campaign appeals to patriotism rather than responding directly to gun-control proposals.

1. The Democrats are conspiring on a new education bill.

2. CEOs waltz away with millions in salary, stock options, and pensions while the little people who keep the company running get peanuts.

3. America is turning into a nation of fatsos.

4. Tree-huggers ranted about the Explorer's gas mileage outside the Ford dealership.

5. If the granola-loving mayor has his way, it will soon be a criminal offense to drink a twenty-ounce soda.

6. Naive voters often stumble to the polls and blithely yank whichever handles are closest to them.

7. Liberals constantly whine about protecting civil rights, but they don't care about protecting the flag that Americans have fought and died for.

8. A mob of protesters appeared, yelling and jabbing their signs in the air.

23.5 Considering connotation

Study the italicized words in each of the following passages, and decide what each word's connotations contribute to your understanding of the passage. Think of a synonym for each word, and see whether you think the new word would affect the passage. (See *The Everyday Writer*, section 23b.) Example:

> It is a story of extended horror. But it isn't only the horror that *numbs* response. Nor is it that the discoverer [Columbus] *deteriorates* so steadily after the discovery. It is the *banality* of the man. He was looking less for America or Asia than for gold; and the banality of expectation matches a continuing banality of *perception.*
> – V. S. NAIPAUL, "Columbus and Crusoe"
>
> *numbs:* deadens, paralyzes
> *deteriorates:* declines, gets worse
> *banality:* ordinariness, triviality
> *perception:* understanding, judgment

1. The Burmans were already *racing* past me across the mud. It was obvious that the elephant would never *rise* again, but he was not dead.

He was breathing very rhythmically with long *rattling* gasps, his great *mound* of a side painfully rising and falling.
> – GEORGE ORWELL, "Shooting an Elephant"

2. Then one evening Miss Glory told me to serve the ladies on the porch. After I set the tray down and turned toward the kitchen, one of the women asked, "What's your name, *girl*?"
> – MAYA ANGELOU, *I Know Why the Caged Bird Sings*

3. We caught two bass, *hauling* them in *briskly* as though they were mackerel, pulling them over the side of the boat in a *businesslike* manner without any landing net, and stunning them with a *blow* on the back of the head.
> – E. B. WHITE, "Once More to the Lake"

4. The Kiowas are a summer people; they *abide* the cold and keep to themselves; but when the season *turns* and the land becomes warm and *vital*, they cannot *hold still*.
> – N. SCOTT MOMADAY, "The Way to Rainy Mountain"

5. If boxing is a sport, it is the most *tragic* of all sports because, more than any [other] human activity, it *consumes* the very excellence it *displays*: Its very *drama* is this consumption.
> – JOYCE CAROL OATES, "On Boxing"

23.6   Using specific and concrete words

Rewrite each of the following sentences to be more specific and more concrete. (See *The Everyday Writer*, section 23c.) Example:

The truck entered the roadway.

The enormous red dump truck, piled high with shiny chunks of asphalt and smelling of hot tar, clambered onto the highway right in front of me, blocking my vision and contaminating my lungs.

1. That book was interesting.

2. She couldn't decide what to eat.

3. I pulled over and waited for the tow truck.

4. The castle is very old.

5. He waited for the bus.

6. Our room was a mess.

7. The children enjoyed the fair.

8. The cake was delicious.

9. Gianna felt nervous about the performance.

10. Tyler likes skateboarding.

23.7 Thinking about similes and metaphors

Identify the similes and metaphors in the following numbered items, and decide how each contributes to your understanding of the passage or sentence in which it appears. (See *The Everyday Writer*, section 23d.) Example:

> **Her strong arms, her kisses, the clean soap smell of her face, her voice calming me—all of this was gone. She was like a statue in a church.**
> **– LOUISE ERDRICH, "Shamengwa"**
>
> *like a statue in a church (simile): vividly emphasizes the woman's cold, stone-like persona*

1. Smell is a potent wizard that transports us across thousands of miles and all the years we have lived.   – HELEN KELLER, *The World I Live In*

2. He sometimes thinks marriage is like a football game and he's quarter-backing the underdog team.   – STEPHEN KING, "Premium Harmony"

3. One fall morning, as she crossed the flattened fields of unharvested wheat, she had the sensation that she was walking on an enormous ash-blond wig, like the one Aunt Vance used to wear.

4. The senses feed shards of information to the brain like microscopic pieces of a jigsaw puzzle.
   – DIANE ACKERMAN, *A Natural History of the Senses*

5. I like cemeteries too because they are huge, densely populated cities.
   – GUY DE MAUPASSANT, "The Graveyard Sisterhood"

6. I remember how the world looked from our sitting-room window as I dressed behind the stove that morning: the low sky was like a sheet of metal; the blond cornfields had faded out into ghostliness at last; the little point was frozen under its stiff willow bushes.
   –WILLA CATHER, *My Ántonia*

7. Leila watched in horror as the train, a great lumbering beast unaware of its own power, slowed but could not stop before crashing into the stalled car.

8. He switched on the light and swung his legs out of bed, feeling shaky and slightly nauseous from the vividness of the memory. It was like malaria, he thought. Like a virus that lingers in the body and returns to haunt you.
   –MARY LAWSON, *The Other Side of the Bridge*

9. Consider the beer can. It was beautiful—as beautiful as the clothespin, as inevitable as the wine bottle, as dignified and reassuring as the fire hydrant.
   –JOHN UPDIKE, "Beer Can"

10. The sun was a wide crescent, like a segment of tangerine.
    –ANNIE DILLARD, "Total Eclipse"

23.8 Recognizing correct spellings

Underline the correct spelling from the pair of words in parentheses in each of the following sentences. (See *The Everyday Writer*, sections 23e and f.) Example:

Have you ever taken the food list (chalenge/<u>challenge</u>)?

1. You can (easily/easyly) find the list online of the 100 foods to eat before you (die/dye).

2. The (foodes/foods) represent a range of culinary tastes and traditions from around the United States and the world.

3. According to some Web (cites/sites), most people have eaten only twenty or fewer of these items.

4. (Their/There) are some unusual items on the list, (includeing/including) crickets, frogs' legs, and kangaroo.

5. My (freinds/friends) and I took the quiz, and I was (surprised/surprized) to see the things they have eaten.

6. They (to/too) were shocked to learn what I had (tried/tryed): venison, squirrel, and rabbit stew, all while spending the summer at my boyfriend's hunting camp.

7. Alicia, who is from Louisiana, was the only one of us who had eaten (fried/fryed) green (tomatoes/tomatos).

8. Alicia (says/sayes) she once had the chance to eat alligator, but that she (passed/past) it up.

9. Ben, from New York, has had most of the (favorites/favorits) of that city, such as borscht, bagels and lox, and a pastrami sandwich.

10. I don't understand why Hostess (fruit/friut) pie is on the list, because most of the other items are fresh or unusual.

23.9 Proofreading for spelling

The following paragraph has already been checked using a word processor's spell checker. Correct any spelling errors that may remain. (See *The Everyday Writer*, sections 23e and f.)

Elisha enjoys writing articles four the school news paper, *Student life.* Each week, she has to tern in a column relating to evens on campus. She tries two cover important topics that students have expressed they're concern about. She has written about security problems inn the dorms, lack off funding for late-night bus service, an the need for moor vegetarian options in the dinning halls. Elisha doesn't get paid for her stores, and she does not receive any college credit for them. She is hopping, thought, that her work at the paper will help her too begin a career in journalism when she gradates form school.

23.10 Distinguishing among homonyms

Choose the appropriate word in each set of parentheses. (See *The Everyday Writer,* section 23e.) Example:

Antifreeze can have a toxic (affect/<u>effect</u>) on pets.

People need antifreeze in (their/there/they're) cars in cold (weather/ whether). Unfortunately, antifreeze also tastes (grate/great) to cats and dogs, who drink it from the greenish puddles commonly (scene/seen) on asphalt. Antifreeze made of ethylene glycol causes kidney failure and has (lead/ led) to the deaths of many pets. (Its/It's) not (to/too/two) hard to protect (your/you're) animals from antifreeze poisoning, however. First, (buy/by) antifreeze that does not contain ethylene glycol, in spite of (its/it's) higher cost. Second, do not let pets wander out of (cite/sight/site) when they are outdoors. Third, if a pet acts sick, get help even if the animal (seams/seems) to improve—animals with antifreeze poisoning appear to feel better shortly before they (die/dye). And finally, give the animal vodka or other liquor as an antidote, but only if (their/there/they're) is no way for a veterinarian to look at your pet immediately.

23.11 Spelling plurals

Form the plural of each of the following words. (See *The Everyday Writer*, section 23f.) Example:

fox *foxes*

1. deer

2. curriculum

3. leech

4. wolf

5. cherry

6. man-of-war

7. echo

8. spy

9. analysis

10. box

11. wish

12. mother-in-law

24.1 Selecting the appropriate word

Choose the appropriate word for each of the following sentences from the pair of words in parentheses. (See *The Everyday Writer*, Chapter 24.) Example:

She looked fragile and (<u>weak</u>/week).

1. The (explicit/implicit) perfume advertisement shocked readers.

2. I am too tired to walk any (farther/further).

3. I was (disinterested/uninterested) in hearing his latest excuse.

4. There are (fewer/less) graduates interested in education (than/then) there used to be.

5. School will be canceled today (due to/because of) inclement weather.

6. I will tell you the story, but please be (discreet/discrete).

7. One (affect/effect) of her stroke was impaired mobility.

8. I was reluctant to (loan/lend) him any more money.

9. We added insulation to the windows to (assure/ensure) that we would not have any drafts.

10. Jill felt (bad/badly) that Jack broke his crown.

11. If only we (could of/could have) stopped him from making that terrible mistake!

12. (Can/May) I have the next dance?

13. The students fully expected to be (censored/censured) by the headmaster for their inappropriate behavior.

14. That (continual/continuous) dripping from the faucet is driving me mad!

15. After (awhile/a while), we forgot the reason we had argued in the first place.

16. My English paper compares the works of Jane Austen (with/to) Charlotte Brontë's.

17. I used to support that candidate, but I cannot stand him (anymore/any more).

18. The way she (flouts/flaunts) her newfound wealth is appalling.

19. Her grades were among the most (distinct/distinctive) in the entire school.

20. She couldn't decide (whether or not/if) she should transfer to a different college.

24.2 Editing inappropriate words

In each of the following sentences, remove or replace inappropriate words. If all the words in a sentence are appropriate, mark the sentence C. (See *The Everyday Writer*, Chapter 24.) Example:

> whose
> Ellie looked at the sink in disgust and wondered who's turn it was to
> ^
> do the dishes.

1. I have completed all the classes I need for my core requirements accept foreign language.

2. Ryan went to the writing center to get some advise on improving his research paper.

3. The rain did not affect the starting time of the lacrosse game.

4. On a sunny day Mt. Rainier gives the allusion of floating in air just south of Seattle.

5. Serena could not choose between the fourteen different flavors of homemade gelato.

6. Quinn felt badly about losing the game, but she knew she had tried her best.

7. Being that exchange rates are so unfavorable right now, James decided to stay in the United States for his vacation.

8. Shows that air on television before 10:00 PM must be censured if they contain profane language.

9. Alex would not leave the restaurant without complimenting the chef in person for the excellent meal.

10. While waiting at the gate for my plane, I was conscience of a suitcase that had been left unattended for more than ten minutes.

11. The instructor could of failed the entire class, but instead he chose to reissue the test.

12. Chloe's parents emigrated from Ireland to the United States in the 1800s.

13. After you pass the stop sign, continue a bit further down the road and you will see our store on the left.

14. There are definitely less cookies on the plate now than there were this morning.

15. After weeks of physical therapy, Gordon can now walk good with a cane.

16. Ideally, a puppy shouldn't be separated from it's mother until it is eight weeks old.

17. Fire was one of the most important discoveries for the development of mankind.

18. The morale of the story is that crime does not pay.

19. We past the exit several miles ago!

20. The reason I canceled my Facebook account was because it interfered with my studying.

Sentence Style

25.1 Combining sentences with coordination

Using the principles of coordination to signal equal importance or to create special emphasis, combine and revise the following ten short sentences into several longer and more effective ones. Add or delete words as necessary. (See *The Everyday Writer,* Chapter 25, especially section 25a.)

The beach was deserted. I wondered where all of the surfers were. The waves were calling to me. The sand was burning my feet. I walked toward the ocean. I let the water splash my ankles. Standing at the water's edge, I watched for a very long time. I knew it was getting late. I had to make my way back. I picked up a few seashells to give to my little sister.

25.2 Writing sentences with subordination

Combine each of the following sets of sentences into one sentence that uses subordination to signal the relationships among ideas. Add or delete words as necessary. (See *The Everyday Writer,* section 25b.) Example:

The Spaniards arrived at the Aztec capital of Tenochtitlan.
They were amazed at the beauty and complexity of the city.
It had been built by people the Spaniards considered inferior to themselves.

When the Spaniards arrived at the Aztec capital of Tenochtitlan, they were amazed at the beauty and complexity of the city, which had been built by people the Spaniards considered inferior to themselves.

1. Brandon is not a sports fan.

    I took him to a baseball game.

    I knew he would enjoy the hot dogs.

2. An umbrella can keep you cool at the beach.

   It can't completely protect you from the sun.

   The rays reflect from the sand onto your skin.

   You still need to wear sunscreen.

3. Steve Jobs founded Apple computers in 1976.

   He was fired in 1985 by the board of directors.

   They didn't agree with his management style.

4. My sister thinks reality television shows are completely unscripted.

   I think many of the people are actually acting.

   The viewers will be drawn in by the drama.

5. I was on the track team in high school.

   I had to stop running in college.

   I injured my knee playing tennis.

25.3 Using coordination and subordination

Revise the following paragraph, using coordination and subordination where appropriate to clarify the relationships among ideas. (See *The Everyday Writer*, Chapter 25, especially sections 25a and b.)

Reggae is a style of music. It originated in Jamaica in the late 1960s. Reggae evolved out of earlier types of Jamaican music. Ska was one of reggae's main influences. It has a fast-paced rhythm. It accents the second and fourth beats of each measure. Ska developed in Jamaica in the late 1950s. It combined elements of calypso music and American jazz and rhythm and blues. Ska led to another form of music known as rocksteady in the mid-1960s. It had a beat similar to ska. Rocksteady focused more on vocal harmonies. Rocksteady's tempo was a bit slower. Ska and rocksteady retained popularity in Jamaica. Reggae emerged within a few years. Reggae eclipsed both of its predecessors. Reggae songs focus on politics and racial equality. They resonated with the youths of the time. Youths of the time were rising up in protest movements around the world. Musicians Bob Marley and Jimmy Cliff became internationally famous in the 1970s. Reggae gained a permanent place in popular music around the world.

25.4 Emphasizing main ideas

Revise each of the following sentences to highlight what you take to be the main or most important ideas. (See *The Everyday Writer*, section 25c.) Example:

> **Science-fiction movies are among the highest-grossing films ever made:**
> ***ET* brought in $435 million, ~~*Avatar* earned over $760 million, and~~ *Dark Knight* grossed over $530 million** , and *Avatar* earned over $760 million.
> ^

1. One major problem is the regular appearance of fire ants in our yard.

2. Ever since the iPhone became popular, apps have been created that allow us to play games, instantly recognize constellations in the night sky, and record voice memos.

3. Large numbers of people don't bother with recycling because it takes up time, uses up storage space, and can lead to unpleasant odors, even though many people agree that recycling is generally beneficial.

4. The word *marathon* comes from the ancient Greek legend that a runner delivered a victory message from the Battle of Marathon to Athens, which was twenty-six miles away, as many people have heard.

5. Although industrial dairy farmers insist that bovine growth hormone is harmless, the public wonders whether it could have strange effects on the human endocrine system, cause cancer, or lead to digestive trouble.

6. Born in Austria in 1756, Mozart is perhaps the greatest composer of all time, having written enduringly popular operas, concertos, and symphonies.

7. Ansel Adams was a photographer, his color photographs were published to critical acclaim after his death, and he was generally known for his stark, black-and-white landscape photographs.

8. The palm tree is not a tree, even though it is tall and appears to have leaves and a trunk.

9. Tim doesn't gamble very often, but he knows that the odds of winning the Powerball jackpot are one in 175 million, slot machines always favor the house, and roulette is difficult to win.

10. This all-in-one plant food I bought led to the largest tomato crop I have ever seen, kept the bugs away, and prevented fungus from forming.

26.1 Matching subjects and predicates

Revise each of the following sentences in two ways to make its structures consistent in grammar and meaning. (See *The Everyday Writer*, section 26b.) Example:

By studying African American folklore and biblical stories have influenced Toni Morrison's fiction.

African American folklore and biblical stories have influenced Toni Morrison's fiction.

Toni Morrison's study of African American folklore and biblical stories has influenced her fiction.

1. Toni Morrison's grandmother, who moved to Ohio from the South with only fifteen dollars to her name, and Morrison had great respect for her.

2. In her books, many of which deal with the aftermath of slavery, often feature strong women characters.

3. Published in 1970, Morrison's first novel, *The Bluest Eye*, the story of a young African American girl who wants to look like her Shirley Temple doll.

4. Although Morrison's depictions of African American families and neighborhoods are realistic, but they also include supernatural elements.

5. An important character in Morrison's 1977 novel *Song of Solomon* is about Pilate, a woman with magical powers.

6. *Song of Solomon*, hailed as a masterpiece, winning the National Book Critics Circle Award in 1978.

7. Morrison's fame as a writer won the Pulitzer Prize in fiction in 1988 for *Beloved*.

8. The title character in *Beloved* features the ghost of a murdered infant inhabiting the body of a young woman.

9. When reading *Beloved* makes the horrors of American slavery seem immediate and real.

10. In 1993, Toni Morrison, who became the first African American woman to be awarded the Nobel Prize in literature.

26.2 Making comparisons complete, consistent, and clear

Revise each of the following sentences to eliminate any inappropriate elliptical constructions; to make comparisons complete, logically consistent, and clear; and to supply any other omitted words that are necessary for meaning. (See *The Everyday Writer*, section 26e.) Example:

> **American soccer (known as football in most of the world) is more**
> it is in
> **popular in Europe than the United States.**
> ^

1. Mira did much better on the history test.

2. Records show that the average sea temperature in the past decade is higher.

3. Britain's Andy Green earned the land speed record in 1997 by driving his jet-propelled vehicle faster than the American.

4. 3-D movies these days are a bit blurry, but they are still better than the 1950s.

5. As the counselor pointed out, some jobs require more education.

6. Travel on a commercial airplane is statistically safer than a car.

7. Heart disease kills more people than cancer.

8. Alligators typically have more teeth than crocodiles.

9. Taking out loans to pay for college may seem financially risky, but forgoing a college education even riskier.

10. Is the U.S. national debt higher than other countries?

26.3 Revising for consistency and completeness

Revise this passage so that all sentences are grammatically and logically consistent and complete. (See *The Everyday Writer,* Chapter 26.)

A concentrated animal feeding operation, or CAFO, is when a factory farm raises thousands of animals in a confined space. Vast amounts of factory-farm livestock waste, dumped into giant lagoons, which are an increasingly common sight in rural areas of this country. Are factory-farm operations healthy for their neighbors, for people in other parts of the country, and the environment? Many people think that these operations damage our air and water more than small family farms.

One problem with factory farming is the toxic waste that has contaminated groundwater in the Midwest. In addition, air quality produces bad-smelling and sometimes dangerous gases that people living near a CAFO have to breathe. When a factory farm's neighbors complain may not be able

to close the operation. The reason is because most factory farms have powerful corporate backers.

Not everyone is angry about the CAFO situation; consumers get a short-
term benefit from a large supply of pork, beef, and chicken that is cheaper
than family farms can raise. However, the more people know about factory
farms, the less interest in supporting their farming practices.

27.1 Creating parallel words or phrases

Complete the following sentences, using parallel words or phrases in
each case. (See *The Everyday Writer*, sections 27a and b.) Example:

> **The wise politician** _promises the possible_ , _effects the unavoidable_ ,
>
> **and** _accepts the inevitable_ .

1. My favorite pastimes include _____ , _____ ,
   and _____ .

2. This summer, I want to _____ , _____ , and
   _____ .

3. My motto is _____ , _____ , and
   _____ .

4. In preparation for his wedding day, the groom _____ ,
   _____ , and _____ .

5. _____ , _____ , and _____
   are activities my grandparents enjoy.

6. When he got his promotion, he _____ , _____ ,
   and _____ .

7. You should _____ , _____ , or
   _____ before you invite six guests for dinner.

8. The college athlete realized she would need to both _____

   and _____ .

9. Graduates find that the job market _____ ,

   _____ , and _____ .

10. Just as _____ , so has _____ .

27.2 Revising sentences for parallelism

Revise the following sentences to eliminate any errors in parallel structure. (See *The Everyday Writer*, Chapter 27.) Example:

> Pérez Prado's orchestra was famous for playing irresistible rhythms
> turning
> and ~~because it turned~~ the mambo into a new dance craze.
> ^

1. The latest dance steps and wearing festive party clothes were necessities for many teenagers in the 1950s.

2. Many people in this country remember how they danced to the mambo music of the 1950s and listening to that era's Latin bands.

3. Older dancers may recall Rosemary Clooney, Perry Como, and Ruth Brown singing mambo numbers and Pérez Prado's band had a huge hit, "Cherry Pink and Apple Blossom White."

4. Growing up near Havana and a student of classical piano, Pérez Prado loved Cuban music.

5. Pérez Prado wanted not only to play Cuban music but also he wanted to combine it with elements of jazz.

6. Playing piano in Havana nightclubs, arranging music for a Latin big band, and the jam sessions he joined with the band's guitarists gave him the idea for a new kind of music.

7. The result was a new dance phenomenon: mambo music was born, and Pérez Prado, who became known as "King of the Mambo."

8. Prado conducted his orchestra with hand waving, head and shoulder movements, and by kicking his feet high in the air.

9. His recordings feature syncopated percussion, wailing trumpets, and Prado shouted rhythmically.

10. Pérez Prado, innovative and a great musician, died in 1989.

27.3 Revising for parallelism and supplying necessary words

Revise the following paragraph to maintain parallelism where it exists and to supply all words necessary for clarity, grammar, and idiom in parallel structures. (See *The Everyday Writer,* Chapter 27.)

Family gatherings for events like weddings, holidays, and going on vacation are supposed to be happy occasions, but for many people, getting together with family members causes tremendous stress. Everyone hopes to share warm memories and for a picture-perfect family event. Unfortunately, the reality may include an uncle who makes offensive remarks, a critical mother, or anger at a spouse who doesn't lift a finger to help. Neither difficult relatives nor when things go wrong will necessarily ruin a big family gathering, however. The trick is to plan for problems and being able to adapt. Family members who are not flexible, not pleasant to be around, or willing to do their part may always be a problem for their relatives. However, people who try to make a family gathering a success will almost always either be able to enjoy the event or laugh about it later.

28.1 Revising for verb tense and mood

Revise any of the following sentences in which you find unnecessary shifts in verb tense or in mood. If a sentence is correct as written, write C. (See *The Everyday Writer*, sections 28a and b.) Examples:

did
I tried using a new cable, but the computer ~~does~~ not turn on.
                                                  ^

When I called the help line, a voice said the wait would be longer
                          that I
than thirty minutes and ~~you~~ should use the online help service
                          ^
instead.

1. If I could use the online help service, that means my computer is working!

2. I waited for almost forty-five minutes on hold, but after a while I give up hope.

3. If I were running my business this way, customers just disappear.

4. In business courses, they teach you that your customer list is your greatest asset and remember that the customer is always right!

5. If you made your customers too upset, they decide to shop elsewhere.

6. It is harder to get customers back than it is to get them in the first place.

7. Customers got especially annoyed when their needs are not being met and the company does not acknowledge these concerns.

8. If their product is defective, why do I waste my time trying to repair it?

9. I am thinking about all this while the annoying music played over the phone line.

10. Finally, I hang up the phone, drove to the computer store, and got my money back.

28.2 Eliminating shifts in voice and point of view

Revise each of the following sentences to eliminate an unnecessary shift in voice or point of view. (See *The Everyday Writer*, sections
28c and d.) Examples:

> When I remember to take deep breaths and count to ten, ~~you~~ really
> can control ~~your~~ anger.

(edits shown: inserted "I" above "you"; "my" above "your")

1. If one has been pleased with a purchase on our site, would you consider
   reviewing it?

2. I had planned to walk home after the movie, but you shouldn't be on
   campus alone after dark.

3. When Occupy protests spread from New York to California, fears of
   possible violence and vandalism were conjured up.

4. Instructors at the studio cooperative offer a wide variety of dance lessons,
   and art and voice training are also given there.

5. Many home-improvement projects are completed by do-it-yourselfers,
   but some people prefer to hire contractors.

6. The twenty-four-hour cable news channel is not all that new; they have
   been around for over thirty years.

7. We knew that emails promising free gifts were usually scams, but you
   couldn't resist clicking on the link just to see.

8. Ziplining lessons were taken by some members of the group while
   others went on a rapids ride.

9. The seedlings could be damaged by a late-spring frost, so we covered
   the flower bed.

10. The slow food movement emerged in France several decades ago; they
    set out to oppose the spread of fast-food chains in Europe.

28.3 Eliminating shifts between direct and indirect discourse

To eliminate the shifts between direct and indirect discourse in the following sentences, put the direct discourse into indirect form. (See *The Everyday Writer*, section 28e.) Example:

> states   his
> Steven Pinker ~~stated~~ that ~~my~~ book is meant for people who use
>   ^   ^
> language and respect it.

1. Richard Rodriguez acknowledges that intimacy was not created by a language; "it is created by intimates."

2. She said that during a semester abroad, "I really missed all my friends."

3. The bewildered neighbor asked him, "What the heck he thought he was doing on the roof?"

4. Loren Eiseley feels an urge to join the birds in their soundless flight, but in the end he knows that he cannot, and "I was, after all, only a man."

5. The instructor told us, "Please read the next two stories before the next class" and that she might give us a quiz on them.

28.4 Eliminating shifts in tone and word choice

Revise each of the following sentences to eliminate shifts in tone and word choice. (See *The Everyday Writer*, section 28f.) Example:

> You should try
> ~~It would behoove you to endeavor~~ to cut down on all those sweets.
> ^

1. Once they start picking up regular gigs, some musicians find that they can afford to stop working a full-time day job.

2. The novel concludes without tying up all of the loose ends, which would be tolerable if the narrator hadn't made me barf with all her nonsensical garbage.

3. In the late 1990s, Starbucks revolutionized the way most Americans grab a cup of joe each day.

4. Once I get sucked into a video game, I find it rather challenging to extricate myself from the sofa.

5. Before Vegas earned a rep for being a total party scene, it was an arid stretch of desert that few people knew existed.

29.1 Eliminating unnecessary words and phrases

Make each of the following sentences clear and concise by eliminating unnecessary words and phrases and by making additions or revisions as needed. (See *The Everyday Writer*, Chapter 29.) Example:

> **The ~~incredible, unbelievable~~ feats that Houdini performed amazed ~~and astounded~~ all of his audiences ~~who came to see him~~.**

1. Harry Houdini, whose real birth name was Ehrich Weiss, made the claim that he had been born in Appleton, Wisconsin, but in actual fact he was born into the world in Budapest, Hungary.

2. Shortly after Houdini's birth, his family moved to Appleton, where his father served as the one and only rabbi in Appleton at that point in time.

3. Houdini gained fame as a really great master escape artist.

4. His many numerous escapes included getting out of a giant sealed envelope without tearing it and walking out of jail cells that were said to be supposedly escape-proof.

5. Before his untimely early death, Houdini told his brother to burn and destroy all papers describing how Houdini's illusions worked.

6. Clearly, it is quite obvious that Houdini did not want anyone at all to know his hidden secrets.

7. Part of the explanation for Houdini's escape artistry lies in the fact that his physique was in absolutely peak physical condition.

8. Houdini's tremendous control over almost every single individual muscle allowed him to contort his body into seemingly impossible positions.

9. After his mother's death, Houdini grew interested in spiritualism until he discovered that the mediums who were the people running the séances were frauds trying to do nothing more than bilk and cheat their customers.

10. On his deathbed, Houdini promised his wife that he would try and attempt to make contact with her from beyond the grave, but so far, he has never been able to get in touch yet.

29.2 Revising for conciseness

Revise the following paragraph so that each sentence is as concise as possible. Combine or divide sentences if necessary. (See *The Everyday Writer*, Chapter 29.)

In this day and age, many people obsess over or dwell on the loss of their youthful appearance when they approach middle age in their thirties and forties. One of the most common professional treatments in the area of skin care is an injection called or known as Botox. Botox contains small amounts of poisonous toxins that deaden the facial muscles that cause wrinkles in the region of the forehead. Collagen injections are another common and widespread treatment that temporarily fill in wrinkles for a limited time. The injection of collagen can also be utilized for the purpose of making lips appear fuller. One thing that cosmetic companies make enormous profits on is specialized creams that do not require a prescription yet promise a more youthful appearance or look. In terms of how they try to attract or entice consumers, some companies put fancy beads, crystals, and even gold into their creams. In spite of the fact that people spend millions of dollars each year on over-the-counter facial creams, the only cream proven to combat wrinkles is a prescription-only cream called tretinoin that must be ordered by a physician. Due to the fact that some people with sensitive skin may have a reaction to tretinoin, users should apply the medication sparingly at first and use sun protection at all times when outside.

30.1 Varying sentence length and structure

The following paragraph can be improved by varying sentence length. Read it aloud to get a sense of how it sounds. Then revise it, creating some short sentences and combining other sentences to create more effective long sentences. Feel free to add words or change punctuation. (See *The Everyday Writer,* Chapter 30.)

One way to determine whether a car is a good value is for a consumer to find out if it will be expensive to maintain, for a car that needs frequent repairs will cost more than a car that does not. Prospective buyers can get statistics detailing the number of repairs needed for various makes and models of cars, and that information can be useful. But the number of repairs alone does not tell the whole story about the overall cost of a car's maintenance, as foreign cars may cost more to repair than domestic cars. Routine maintenance such as oil changes can cost more on an import, and parts that have to be ordered from distant places can be quite expensive. A buyer may know the number and cost of repairs of a particular car, yet he or she may still encounter surprises. Sometimes a car that is not an especially reliable model may run for thousands of miles with very little maintenance, and the owner will be delighted. The converse is also true, and sometimes a car from a company with an excellent reputation may be in the shop more than on the road. Consumers are better off doing their homework than trusting to instinct when buying a car, but luck will still play a role.

Sentence Grammar

31.1 Identifying subjects and predicates

The following sentences are taken from "A Hanging" and "Shooting an Elephant," two essays by George Orwell. Identify the complete subject and the complete predicate in each sentence, underlining the subject once and the predicate twice. (See *The Everyday Writer*, sections 31j and k.) Example:

They **were going to have their bit of fun after all.**

1. His mouth slobbered.

2. It was an immense crowd, two thousand at the least and growing every minute.

3. One could have imagined him thousands of years old.

4. In a job like that, you see the dirty work of Empire at close quarters.

5. All this was perplexing and upsetting.

6. The hangman, a gray-haired convict in the white uniform of the prison, was waiting beside his machine.

7. The dog answered the sound with a whine.

8. Would I please come and do something about it?

9. And at that distance, peacefully eating, the elephant looked no more dangerous than a cow.

10. We set out for the gallows.

31.2 Identifying verbs and verb phrases

Underline each verb or verb phrase in the following sentences. (See *The Everyday Writer*, section 31b.) Example:

Many cultures <u>celebrate</u> the arrival of spring with a festival of some kind.

1. The spring festival of Holi occurs in northern India every March during the full moon.

2. Holi is known as the festival of colors, not only because spring brings flowers, but also because Holi celebrations always include brightly colored dyes.

3. According to legend, the festival of colors began thousands of years ago when Krishna played pranks on girls in his village and threw water on them.

4. During Holi, people toss fistfuls of powdered dyes or dye-filled water balloons at each other and sing traditional Holi songs.

5. Holi festivals allow people freedoms that would be unthinkable during the rest of the year.

6. Any person who is walking outside during a Holi celebration will soon be wearing colored powders or colored water.

7. Men, women, and children can throw powders or dye-filled balloons at anyone, even if the person is much older or of much higher status than they are.

8. Some people wear white clothing for Holi.

9. By the end of the celebration, the white clothes are a riot of color.

10. Doesn't Holi sound like fun?

31.3 Identifying nouns and articles

Identify the nouns, including possessive forms, and the articles in each of the following sentences. Underline the nouns once and the articles twice. (See *The Everyday Writer*, sections 31c and 58d.) Example:

Whitney's favorite **book** has been on **the** **list** of **best-sellers** for over **a** **year**.

1. Slavery existed long before the colonization of America.

2. Will you please turn down the music while I am studying?

3. An animated film may employ hundreds of artists.

4. I have to write four papers this semester, but I don't have any final exams.

5. Life on a farm requires patience and hard work.

6. In the United States at the end of the twentieth century, most people did not own a cell phone, a personal computer, or a digital camera.

7. The leading brands of orange juice are produced from a combination of foreign and domestic fruit.

8. In Harry Potter's world, owls deliver the mail and goblins control the bank.

9. Doctors are not sure what causes autism.

10. A plasma television uses power even when it is not turned on.

31.4 Identifying pronouns and antecedents

Identify the pronouns and any antecedents in each of the following sentences, underlining the pronouns once and any antecedents twice. (See *The Everyday Writer*, section 31d.) Example:

A guide dog must handle **itself** well in any situation.

1. Everyone has seen a guide dog at some time in his or her life.

2. Guide dogs that work with the blind must act as their human partners' eyes.

3. These dogs learn socialization and basic obedience training when they are puppies.

4. Knowing they will have to give up their dog one day, sighted volunteers agree to live with and train a puppy for the first year of its life.

5. Puppies that are destined to be guide dogs are allowed t ɔ go into places that routinely refuse entry to other kinds of dogs.

6. If you see a puppy in a supermarket or an office, loo ⸴ for its special coat that identifies it as a trainee guide dog.

7. Volunteer trainers miss their pups after the train.ng period ends, but nothing is more rewarding than knowing that .he pups will make life easier for their new owners.

8. Some of the pups do not pass the requirements to become guide dogs, but these are in great demand as household pets.

9. When a dog passes the test and graduates, it and its blind companion learn to work with each other during an intensive training session.

10. If you are interested in learning about guide dogs or in becoming a volunteer, contact your local school for the blind.

31.5 Identifying adjectives and adverbs

Identify the adjectives and adverbs in each of the following sentences, underlining the adjectives once and the adverbs twice. Remember that articles and some pronouns can function as adjectives. (See *The Everyday Writer*, sections 31e and f.) Example:

> The grand piano waited silently and patiently on the stage.

1. Meerkats are exceptionally social creatures.

2. After spending nearly twenty years in prison, the wrongfully accused man was released.

3. We could not resist choosing the smallest and quietest puppy in the litter.

4. Moreover, some talk-show hosts intentionally bait the audience with misleading information.

5. My only requirement for a new apartment is a walk-in closet.

6. Color laser printers are not very expensive, but the ink costs will empty your wallet.

7. Because of the latest round of construction, it is not safe to drink the water.

8. The rusty old swing set is being dismantled.

9. The tortoise slowly made its way across the road as cars artfully dodged the ancient creature.

10. Joelle is quite handy with landscaping equipment.

31.6 Adding adjectives and adverbs

Expand each of the following sentences by adding appropriate adjectives and adverbs. Delete *the* if need be. (See *The Everyday Writer*, sections 31e and f.) Example:

Then three   thoroughly   nervous
~~The~~ veterinarians examined the patient.
  ^   ^   ^   ^

1. Our assignment is due Wednesday.

2. Most of us enjoy movies.

3. Her superiors praised her work for the Environmental Protection Agency.

4. A corporation can fire workers.

5. The heroine marries the prince.

6. The boardwalk crosses the beach.

7. I have neglected my friend.

8. The media are ignoring his candidacy.

9. Nobody saw the bear, but the ranger said it was dangerous.

10. Which way did you say the pair went?

31.7 Identifying prepositions

Underline the prepositions in the following sentences. (See *The Everyday Writer,* section 31g.) Example:

> <u>According to</u> Greek mythology, Cronus presided <u>over</u> the heavens and the earth <u>during</u> the Golden Age.

1. Ares, the god of war, was known for charging into battle without any forethought.

2. Actaeon stumbled upon the pool where Artemis was bathing, and the goddess changed him into a stag as a punishment.

3. Metis turned into a fly and Zeus swallowed her, so she took up residence in his head.

4. Due to Zeus's complaints of constant headaches, Hephaestus split through his skull with an axe.

5. Upon this, Athena emerged, fully grown, from her father's head.

6. In spite of Hera's jealousy, Zeus often came down from Mt. Olympus to visit the mortal women who lived below.

7. Paris sailed across the sea toward Troy out of desire for the beautiful Helen.

8. Huge branches laden with fruit hung above the head of Tantalus, but whenever he reached up to grab them, they moved beyond his reach.

9. In the story of Persephone, Hades tells Demeter that her daughter must live with him beneath the earth for three months each year.

10. From Mt. Olympus, Zeus spied the beautiful Danae, and he descended upon her in the form of a rain shower.

31.8 Identifying conjunctions

Underline the coordinating, correlative, and subordinating conjunctions as well as the conjunctive adverbs in each of the following sentences. Draw a connecting line to show both parts of any correlative conjunctions. (See *The Everyday Writer*, section 31h.) Example:

> Even though the electricity was restored, we turned on
> neither the lights nor the television.

1. Trina speaks both English and German, yet her first language is Arabic.

2. Not only did the big box electronics store force our local store out of business, but it also closed within six months and left many people out of work.

3. Crocodiles usually live in fresh water; nevertheless, they can survive and even thrive in salt water.

4. When the movie ended and the lights came up, we saw many people in the theater wiping their eyes.

5. We were offered either a small table by the door or an even smaller table by the kitchen; therefore, we decided to eat somewhere else.

6. The economy is improving, but millions are still out of work and home values are still low across the country.

7. Should I have the fish or the chicken?

8. The banks will either charge fees to retailers or make the cardholders pay in order to make their profits.

9. Because of rising fuel costs, airline fares have increased.

10. After doing all the dishes, vacuuming the living room, and changing all the sheets, I couldn't decide whether to go to the gym or take a nap.

31.9 Identifying conjunctions and interjections

Underline conjunctions once and interjections twice in each of the following sentences. Write COORD (for coordinating), CORREL (for correlative), or SUBORD (for subordinating) in parentheses after each sentence to indicate the types of conjunctions in use. (See *The Everyday Writer*, sections 31h and i.) Example:

<u>Whoops</u> — <u>when</u> I dropped your teacup, it broke. (SUBORD)

1. Ah, the enticing aroma of gingerbread always makes me feel as if I should have saved room for dessert!

2. Although I prefer cats, I wouldn't mind getting a dog.

3. Jake and Sandy, Elly and Hank, and Sally Jo and Michael all plan to travel together and attend the conference.

4. I stubbed my toe on the nail after I hit my head on the beam. Ouch!

5. Before you order dessert, make sure you have enough money to cover it.

6. Until I saw that movie, I never thought about daily life at that time.

7. The rain kept me from mowing the lawn, but I didn't really mind.

8. Aha! I always suspected they were planning a surprise party, but now I know for sure.

9. If you save money, you'll feel better both now and later.

10. Our parts shipment did not arrive yesterday, so I cannot fill your order.

31.10 Identifying the parts of speech

For each underlined word in the following sentences, write its part of speech as it is used in the sentence. (See *The Everyday Writer,* sections 31a–i.) Example:

pron (indef)   adj   noun

<u>Anybody</u> who has ever taken a <u>standardized</u> <u>test</u> is familiar with

number-two pencils.

1. <u>Common</u> pencils range from number one, <u>which</u> are extra soft and

   black, to number four, which are extra hard <u>and</u> fine.

2. <u>Although</u> <u>we</u> refer to the dark center <u>of</u> the pencil as the "lead," it is <u>not</u>

   made from the element lead.

3. <u>Instead</u>, pencil "leads" have <u>always</u> been made <u>from</u> graphite.

4. A <u>large</u> deposit of <u>exceptionally</u> pure graphite was discovered in

   <u>England</u> in the middle of the sixteenth century, and locals <u>used</u> it for

   marking sheep.

5. <u>Because</u> the field of chemistry was not <u>very</u> advanced, <u>many</u> believed

   that the graphite was actually lead.

6. <u>The</u> term "lead" <u>continues</u> to be used to this day.

7. It <u>took</u> decades to perfect the <u>technique</u> of encasing the graphite in wood

   for ease of use.

8. <u>It</u> was another hundred years <u>before</u> erasers were added to the tips.

9. Some of the best graphite in the world was located in Siberia, <u>so</u> some

   original pencil <u>manufacturers</u> painted the exterior of <u>their</u> pencils yellow

   to represent Asia.

10. <u>Incidentally</u>, many pencil users <u>did contract</u> lead poisoning in the past, but <u>this</u> condition was the result of handling or chewing on the <u>lead</u> paint of the exterior, not the graphite "lead."

31.11 Identifying subjects

Identify the complete subject and the simple subject in each sentence. Underline the complete subject once and the simple subject twice. (See *The Everyday Writer*, section 31j.) Example:

In America, <u>the <u>sport</u> of soccer</u> is less popular than it is in other countries around the world.

1. The origins of soccer, also called football, trace back to almost every corner of the globe.

2. Ancient Chinese, Greeks, and Romans, as well as South and Central Americans, all played versions of "football."

3. Modern-day soccer really began to develop in England in the late nineteenth century.

4. In 1863, eleven London soccer clubs sent their representatives to the Freemason's Tavern for a meeting.

5. Their intended goal was the establishment of a uniform set of guidelines for the sport.

6. In the minority were the proponents of rugby, who were against rules that forbade ball carrying.

7. They did not ultimately have their way.

8. The historical meeting led to the eventual split between rugby and football, and to the founding of the Football Association.

9. The major tournament in professional soccer is the international World

    Cup, which is held every four years.

10. It is the most widely watched sporting event in the world.

31.12 Identifying predicates

Underline the predicate in the following sentences. Then label each verb as linking (LV), transitive (TV), or intransitive (IV). Finally, label all subject (SC) and object (OC) complements and all direct (DO) and indirect (IO) objects. (See *The Everyday Writer*, section 31k.) Example:

$$\overbrace{}^{TV} \overbrace{}^{DO}$$

In the early 1990s, researchers <u>studied</u> <u>the effects of classical music on the brain</u>.

1. Before playing any music, psychologists gave subjects a test on spatial

    reasoning.

2. Then they retested the subjects after playing music by Mozart.

3. Most subjects scored higher on the tests after being exposed to the

    classical music.

4. The psychologists published their findings about the effects of the music

    in a scholarly journal.

5. Then the popular press exaggerated the story.

6. Newspapers and magazines fed people stories about the amazing

    intelligence-boosting properties of classical music.

7. Parents became obsessed with exposing their babies and young children

    to the music of Mozart, Beethoven, and Bach.

8. An entire industry of classical music CD collections, videos, and guide-

    books was born.

9. However, the original researchers were not happy about the oversimplification of their study.

10. They rejected the commercialization of their findings.

31.13 Identifying prepositional phrases

Identify and underline all of the prepositional phrases. Then choose two of the sentences, and for each, write a sentence that imitates its structure. (See *The Everyday Writer*, section 31l.) Example:

He glanced <u>about the room</u> <u>with a cocky, crooked grin</u>.

The cat stalked around the yard in her quiet, arrogant way.

1. He decided to travel across the ocean to America in search of a better life.

2. He sailed from Italy in an overcrowded boat, but he was happy to be among his countrymen and women.

3. Upon his arrival in this country, he was taken immediately to Ellis Island.

4. Without any formal education and against all odds, he learned English and prospered in business.

5. Even after sixty years in this country, he is still a proud Italian American.

31.14 Using prepositional phrases

Combine each of the following pairs of sentences into one sentence by using one or more prepositional phrases. (See *The Everyday Writer*, section 31l.) Example:

with
Teflon is a slippery material./It has many industrial and household uses.
^

1. Teflon was invented in 1938. The inventor was Dr. Roy J. Plunkett.

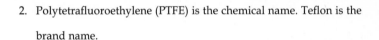

2. Polytetrafluoroethylene (PTFE) is the chemical name. Teflon is the brand name.

3. The benefits of PTFE were immediately obvious. Many scientists understood them.

4. The substance allows food to cook in a pan. The food does not stick.

5. Teflon is not supposed to stick to anything. There is one exception, the pan.

6. Early nonstick cookware coating tended to peel off the surface of the pan. The slightest touch of a metal utensil could remove it.

7. The surface of cookware must be roughened. Then a PTFE primer is applied.

8. The primer holds the PTFE coat in place. A physical bond, not a chemical one, keeps the PTFE on the pan.

9. This slippery substance has kitchen uses. It also protects fabrics from stains.

10. The word *Teflon* can be an adjective. It describes a person who seems to get out of sticky situations easily.

31.15 Identifying verbal phrases

Identify and name each participial phrase, gerund phrase, and infinitive phrase in the following sentences. Identify any sentence in which the verbal phrase acts as the subject of the sentence. (See *The Everyday Writer*, section 31l.) Example:

$$\overline{\qquad\qquad \text{subject} \qquad\qquad}$$
Blogging about a personal goal or topic of concern has exploded in
⌞ gerund ⌟
popularity over the past decade.

1. Writing about oneself in a public forum became accessible to the masses when sites such as Blogger.com and Blogspot.com arose.

2. It is now commonplace for people to write articles about their lives and publish them online.

3. Some bloggers write about losing weight, training for marathons, and trying to get pregnant.

4. Without searching very hard, you can find blogs inspired by military service, blogs focused on careers, and blogs dedicated to cooking.

5. More recently, Facebook has created an enormous network for people to share their thoughts and interests with others.

6. Some people think of Facebook as a collection of miniature blogs, targeted to a specific audience of readers who are known and trusted.

7. Sharing so much online allows us to stay in touch with faraway friends and relatives, but can it be emotionally harmful?

8. Psychologists are investigating whether spending too much time online may lead to a lack of face-to-face relationships.

9. A lack of personal contact and socialization can cause a person to become lonely or depressed.

10. We need to balance our online worlds with our real worlds in order to have a healthy and realistic outlook on life.

31.16 Identifying prepositional, verbal, absolute, and appositive phrases

Read the following sentences, and identify and label all the prepositional, verbal, absolute, and appositive phrases. Notice that one kind of phrase may appear within another kind. (See *The Everyday Writer,* section 31l.) Example:

```
        ┌──────── absolute ────────┐              ┌── prep ──┐
        His voice breaking with emotion, Ed thanked us for the award.
                       └── prep ──┘
              └── verbal ──┘
```

1. To listen to Patsy Cline is sheer delight.

2. The figure outlined against the sky seemed unable to move.

3. Their tails wagging furiously, the dogs at the shelter worked to win new homes.

4. Jane stood still, her fingers clutching the fence.

5. The moviegoers hissed as the villain enticed the child's dog, a Yorkshire terrier, into his car.

6. Floating on my back, I ignored my practice requirements.

7. His favorite form of recreation was taking a nap.

8. Anna, the leader of the group, was reluctant to relinquish any authority.

9. The sun reflected off the magnificent thunderheads, signaling an approaching storm.

10. Shocked into silence, they kept their gaze fixed on the odd creature.

31.17 Adding prepositional, verbal, absolute, and appositive phrases

Use prepositional, participial, infinitive, gerund, absolute, or appositive phrases to expand each of the following sentences. (See *The Everyday Writer*, section 31l.) Example:

> Puffed up like a peacock on parade,
> **Jose approached the stage and accepted his award.**
> ^

1. The tree looked beautiful.

2. The actress ran for political office.

3. The dog growled at the empty foyer.

4. Brent's car won the soap box derby.

5. The runner managed to cross the finish line.

6. Melissa was not accepted into Yale.

7. The space shuttle ascended into space.

8. We attended the convention.

9. I was annoyed with my sister.

10. I decided it would interfere with my schoolwork.

31.18 Using verbal, absolute, and appositive phrases to combine sentences

Use a participial, infinitive, gerund, absolute, or appositive phrase to combine each of the following pairs of sentences into one sentence. (See *The Everyday Writer,* section 31l.) Example:

His constant complaining
~~He complained constantly. This habit~~ irritated his co-workers.
^

1. Ireland is known as the Emerald Isle. It is a magical place to visit.

2. Plan to fly into Dublin. You can backpack your way around the country from there.

3. It is easy to find a central hostel. Consult the Internet or a travel guide before you go.

4. Visit the Ballsbridge area. It is home to foreign embassies and many other sites.

5. Dublin Castle was rebuilt many times over the centuries. It was originally a Viking fortress.

6. The Irish National Gallery is worth checking out for art lovers. It is located at Merrion Square West.

7. The James Joyce museum is outside Dublin. It would be a mistake to skip it.

8. You can stand on the Martello Tower in Sandycove. The Irish Sea is in front of it.

9. A long day of sightseeing is tiring. You will have many authentic pubs to choose from.

10. It will be difficult to say good-bye to Dublin. There is much more of the country to explore.

31.19 Identifying dependent clauses

Underline the dependent clauses, and label any subordinating conjunctions and relative pronouns in each of the following sentences. (See *The Everyday Writer*, section 31m.) Example:

┌rel pron┐
The Appalachian Trail, <u>which stretches from Georgia to Maine</u>, is over 2,100 miles long.

1. Hikers who attempt to walk the whole length of the Appalachian Trail have to put their lives on hold for several months.

2. Most of these hikers start in Georgia when spring arrives in the South.

3. Hikers have to carry all essentials with them because most of the trail meanders through forested mountains far from any towns.

4. Although the Appalachian mountain range has relatively low peaks, they are still a formidable barrier for foot travelers.

5. If a hilly trek with a forty-pound backpack does not sound like a vacation to you, you probably should think twice about taking on the Appalachian Trail.

6. Because the Appalachian Trail lies mainly in wilderness, wild animals are abundant.

7. Many hikers enjoy seeing animals in the wild unless they have a frightening encounter with a bear.

8. Bears that have become accustomed to humans may be a threat to hikers.

9. These bears have learned that people on the Appalachian Trail usually carry plenty of food.

10. Before leaving home, hikers should learn how to react to an aggressive bear to minimize the danger.

31.20 Adding dependent clauses

Expand each of the following sentences by adding at least one dependent clause to it. Be prepared to explain how your addition improves the sentence. (See *The Everyday Writer*, section 31m.) Example:

> who think they are the center of the universe
> **Spoiled children can drive even their parents crazy.**
> ^

1. Working parents may see their children only at the end of the day.

2. Everyone in a family may have high expectations for time together.

3. Children can easily learn how to manipulate their parents.

4. Whining is difficult to listen to and easy to stop with a new toy or an extra video viewing.

5. However, bribing a child to behave better is a flawed technique.

6. Misbehaving children wear out their welcome quickly.

7. Kids should learn that the world does not revolve around their whims.

8. Parents must learn to stick to their own rules.

9. Enforcing rules sometimes worries parents more than it bothers their children.

10. Even if children protest against discipline, they want to know how to behave.

31.21 Distinguishing between phrases and clauses

The following are some sentences from the letters of E. B. White. Read each one carefully, focusing on the phrases and clauses. Underline any dependent clauses once and any phrases twice. Identify each phrase as a prepositional phrase or a verbal phrase. Finally, choose two sentences, and use them as a model for sentences of your own, imitating White's structure phrase for phrase and clause for clause. (See *The Everyday Writer*, sections 31l and m.) Example:

> **I was born <u>in 1899</u> and expect <u>to live forever,</u> <u>searching for beauty</u> and**
>
> **<u>raising hell</u> <u>in general</u>.**
>
> **PREPOSITIONAL PHRASES:** in 1899, for beauty, in general
> **VERBAL PHRASES:** to live forever, searching for beauty, raising hell
> **IMITATION SENTENCE:** Sarah was hired in May and plans to work all summer, living at home and saving money for law school.

1. Either Macmillan takes Strunk and me in our bare skins, or I want out.

2. I regard the word *hopefully* as beyond recall.

3. Life in a zoo is just the ticket for some animals and birds.

4. I recall the pleasures and satisfactions of encountering a Perelman piece in a magazine.

5. The way to read Thoreau is to enjoy him—his enthusiasms, his acute perception.

6. You can see at a glance that Professor Strunk omitted needless words.

7. A good many of Charlotte's descendants still live in the barn, and when the warm days of spring arrive there will be lots of tiny spiders emerging into the world.

8. When I start a book, I never know what my characters are going to do, and I accept no responsibility for their eccentric behavior.

9. No sensible writer sets out deliberately to develop a style, but all writers do have distinguishing qualities, and they become very evident when you read the words.

10. When I wrote "Death of a Pig," I was simply rendering an account of what actually happened on my place —to my pig, who died, and to me, who tended him in his last hours.

31.22 Classifying sentences grammatically and functionally

Classify each of the following sentences as simple, compound, complex, or compound-complex. In addition, note any sentences that could be classified as declarative, imperative, interrogative, or exclamatory. (See *The Everyday Writer*, sections 31n and o.) Example:

Stop the thief! simple, imperative

1. During your semester abroad, keep in touch with your family and friends by mail, email, telephone, or even Pony Express if necessary.

2. When I first arrived at college, I became confused about where I fit in and who my role models should be.

3. People go on safari to watch wild animals in their natural habitat.

4. The woman who moved into the apartment next door to mine let her band practice in the living room, but I would not have moved if their music had not been so boring.

5. Should he admit his mistake, or should he keep quiet and hope to avoid discovery?

6. The screen door creaked and banged when she ran into the house.

7. Solve your problems yourself.

8. Retail sales declined as consumers cut back on spending, and many small businesses failed.

9. Why do people insist on drinking coffee when tea tastes so much better?

10. Oh, I detest jokes at other people's expense!

32.1 Using irregular verb forms

Complete each of the following sentences by filling in each blank with the past tense or past participle of the verb listed in parentheses. (See *The Everyday Writer*, section 32c.) Example:

Frida Kahlo ____*became*____ **(become) one of Mexico's foremost painters.**

1. Frida Kahlo _____ (grow) up in Mexico City, where she _____ (spend) most of her life.

2. She _____ (be) born in 1907, but she often _____ (say) that her birth year _____ (be) 1910.

3. In 1925 a bus accident _____ (leave) Kahlo horribly injured.

4. The accident _____ (break) her spinal column and many other bones, so Kahlo _____ (lie) in bed in a body cast for months.

5. She had always _____ (be) a spirited young woman, and she _____ (take) up painting to avoid boredom while convalescing.

6. Kahlo _____ (meet) the painter Diego Rivera in 1928 and
   _____ (fall) in love; they married the following year.

7. From the beginning, Rivera had _____ (know) that Kahlo's
   work was remarkable, so he encouraged her to paint.

8. Kahlo _____ (keep) working even though she
   _____ (be) in constant pain for the rest of her life.

9. Kahlo usually _____ (choose) to paint self-portraits;
   scholars have _____ (begin) to analyze her unflinching
   vision of herself.

10. The fame of Frida Kahlo has _____ (grow) and
    _____ (spread) since her death in 1954.

32.2 **Editing verb forms**

Where necessary, edit the following sentences to eliminate any inappropriate verb forms. If the verb forms in a sentence are appropriate as written, write C. (See *The Everyday Writer,* section 32c.) Example:

> chose
> **He ~~choosed~~ the fish at the restaurant.**
>   ^

1. Be careful not to burnt the toast!

2. She have went to visit her grandparents in Florida.

3. I was so embarrassed that I hunged my head in shame.

4. She thought she was right, but I proved her wrong.

5. James Bond likes his martinis shooken, not stirred.

6. I have always knew you are a good friend.

7. He waked up in totally unfamiliar surroundings.

8. After I swum the race, I was ready for a hearty breakfast.

9. By the time we woke up, the sun had already risen.

10. I wish you had never lend him the money.

32.3 Distinguishing between *lie* and *lay*, *sit* and *set*, *rise* and *raise*

Choose the appropriate verb form in each of the following sentences. (See *The Everyday Writer*, section 32d.) Example:

The boys laid/<u>lay</u> on the couch, hoping for something good on TV.

1. That politician believes people should rise/raise themselves up by their bootstraps.

2. The little girl laid/lay her head on her mother's shoulder and went to sleep.

3. The students sat/set their backpacks down beside their desks and stared grimly at the new teacher.

4. Sit/Set down and stay awhile.

5. After he died, all the flags were risen/raised to half mast.

6. Don't just lie/lay there; do something!

7. Sitting/Setting in the sun too long can lead to skin cancer.

8. I could really use a rise/raise in pay this time of year.

9. She always lies/lays my fears to rest.

10. As soon as the sun rose/raised, I went for a run.

32.4 Deciding on verb tenses

Complete each of the following sentences by filling in the blank with an appropriate form of the verb given in parentheses. Because more than one form will sometimes be possible, choose one form and then be prepared to explain the reasons for your choice. (See *The Everyday Writer*, section 32e.) Example:

People ___have been practicing/have practiced___ **(practice) the art of**

yoga for thousands of years.

**The present perfect progressive tense *have been practicing* is appropri-
ate because the sentence refers to ongoing action begun in the past
and continuing into the present. The present perfect tense *have prac-
ticed* is also suitable because it is used to indicate actions begun in
the past and either completed at some unspecified time in the past or
continuing into the present.**

1. The word *yoga* _____ (come) from Sanskrit, one of the

   world's most ancient languages.

2. Although many people today _____ (begin) a yoga

   practice purely for physical exercise, it is actually a path to spirituality

   that _____ (date) back thousands and thousands of

   years.

3. Yoga's popularity in the United States _____ (explode)

   over the last decade.

4. As a result of this surge in popularity, many yoga studios

   _____ (open) throughout the city.

5. When you _____ (begin) a yoga practice, it is important

   to find a reputable teacher who _____ (receive) proper

   certification.

6. She _____ (look) for a gentle introduction to yoga, so I

   _____ (suggest) Hatha.

7. The yogi B. K. S. Iyengar _____ (develop) Iyengar yoga in

   the 1930s, and there _____ (be) many Iyengar institutes

   throughout the world today.

8. If you _____ (search) for a more vigorous workout, Vinyasa

   _____ (require) more active movement.

9. The teacher at that studio _____ (be) the best one I

   _____ (see) yet.

10. I _____ (check) out the class schedule for next week to see if

    she _____ (teach).

32.5 Sequencing tenses

Change the italicized word or phrase in each of the following sentences to create the appropriate sequence of tenses. If a sentence reads acceptably, write C. (See *The Everyday Writer*, section 32f.) Example:

> have sent
> **He needs *to send* in his application before today.**
>   ^

1. The girls *will have eaten* breakfast before they went running.

2. Until I started knitting again last month, I *have forgotten* how.

3. *Having sung* in the shower, he did not hear the doorbell.

4. After Darius said that he wanted to postpone college, I *am trying* to talk him out of it.

5. Will she see her old boyfriend when she *had come* home at Thanksgiving?

6. I *have imagined* the job would be finished by this point.

7. You *will have finished* your paper by the time the semester ends.

8. When he was twenty-one, he *wanted to have become* a millionaire by the age of thirty.

9. The news had just begun when our power *goes* out.

10. *Working* at the law firm for five years, she was ready for a change.

32.6   Converting the voice of a sentence

Convert each sentence from active to passive voice or from passive to active, and note the differences in emphasis these changes make. (See *The Everyday Writer,* section 32g.) Example:

The largest fish was caught by me.

   <u>I caught the largest fish.</u>

1.   The car dealerships were overrun by customers during the sale.

2.   Campus security mistreated the protesting students.

3.   The defenseless settlers at Sand Creek were brutally attacked by U.S. soldiers in 1864.

4.   My favorite dinner was cooked by my mother on my birthday.

5.   The lead part in the school play was gotten by Ivan.

6.   An unusual weather pattern is causing storms all across the country.

7.   Several priceless paintings were stolen from the museum by unknown thieves.

8.   The captain ordered the flight attendants to take their seats.

9.   A new novel is being written by J. K. Rowling.

10.   The nurse took my blood pressure.

32.7   Using subjunctive mood

Revise any of the following sentences that do not use the appropriate subjunctive verb forms required in formal or academic writing. If the verb forms in a sentence are appropriate as printed, write C. (See *The Everyday Writer,* section 32h.) Example:

were
If money ~~was~~ no object, I would have one house in the mountains,
         ^
one on the beach, and one in the city.

1. The only requirement is that all applicants are over eighteen years of age.

2. Malcolm is acting as if he was the only one who worked on the project.

3. The host requested that all guests wear name tags.

4. Even if the rain was to stop, it is much too late now to begin the game.

5. If she would have gone to the doctor sooner, the treatments would not be so severe.

6. I wish I was five inches taller.

7. Louisa is packing up her room already, as though she was going to leave before the end of exams.

8. It is necessary that the lender tells you about the terms of your loan in plain language.

9. Maya's brother treats her as if she was his maid.

10. It is a Japanese custom that you should not wear outdoor shoes inside the house.

33.1 Selecting verbs that agree with their subjects

Underline the appropriate verb form in each of the following sentences. (See *The Everyday Writer,* Chapter 33.) Example:

Bankers, politicians, and philanthropists alike is/<u>are</u> becoming increasingly interested in microfinance.

1. Many microlending institutions has/have been in existence since the 1970s.

2. In microlending, small loans is/are provided to poor entrepreneurs in developing nations.

3. These borrowers do/does not possess the collateral required for more traditional loans.

4. Many microlenders has/have made women the primary recipients of their loans.

5. Microloans offer/offers more than just a handout; they promote long-term economic development.

6. Bangladeshi economist Muhammad Yunus is/are considered to be one of the pioneers of the microlending revolution.

7. The Grameen Bank, which Yunus founded in 1976, extend/extends banking services to the poor.

8. Yunus, along with Grameen Bank, was/were the recipient of the 2006 Nobel Peace Prize.

9. A recently published list of the greatest entrepreneurs of all time include/includes Bill Gates, Henry Ford, Benjamin Franklin, and Dr. Yunus.

10. These days, everybody has/have the chance to become an investor through Internet microlending organizations.

33.2 Making subjects and verbs agree

Revise the following sentences as necessary to establish subject-verb agreement. If a sentence does not require any change, write C. (See *The Everyday Writer,* Chapter 33.) Example:

> has
> **A new museum displaying O. Winston Link's photographs ~~have~~**
> ^
> **opened in Roanoke, Virginia.**

1. Anyone interested in steam locomotives have probably already heard of the photographer O. Winston Link.

2. Imagine that it are the 1950s, and Link is creating his famous photographs.

3. The steam locomotives—the "iron horses" of the nineteenth century— has begun to give way to diesel engines.

4. Only the Norfolk & Western rail line's Appalachian route still use steam engines.

5. Link, a specialist in public relations, is also a commercial photographer and train lover.

6. He and his assistant Thomas Garver sets up nighttime shots of steam locomotives.

7. Days of setup is required for a single flash photo of a train passing by.

8. Many of the photos show scenes that would have been totally in the dark without Link's flashbulbs.

9. Up to sixteen flashbulbs and specialized reflectors illuminates every important detail.

10. Link's fine photographic eye and his ability to imagine how the flash will look allows him to compose each photo in advance in the dark.

11. His book *Steam, Steel, and Stars* include most of his stunning nighttime train photographs.

12. Famous Link photos, such as one of a steam engine passing a drive-in movie, appear in the book.

13. Today, the photographs of O. Winston Link has a cult following.

14. More than two thousand negatives from the steam locomotive era belongs to the O. Winston Link Museum in Roanoke.

15. Almost everyone who has seen a Link photograph remembers it.

34.1 Using subjective case pronouns

Replace the underlined noun or nouns in each of the following sentences with the appropriate subjective case pronoun. (See *The Everyday Writer*, section 34a.) Example:

          he
Cameron and ~~Johathan~~ left class early to catch their flight.
         ^

1. Few people could believe that it was <u>Malina</u> who had cleaned the common room.

2. That vacuum cleaner has never worked properly; <u>that vacuum cleaner</u> starts to smoke after five minutes of use.

3. After four hours of searching for the missing watch, <u>Holly, Brendan, and Chelsea</u> decided to give up.

4. Jacqueline and I have completed our survey, and <u>Jacqueline and I</u> are pleased to report our findings.

5. Black racer snakes are not poisonous, but if <u>black racer snakes</u> sense danger or feel cornered, <u>black racer snakes</u> may attack.

6. Katharine Hepburn once said that <u>Katharine Hepburn</u> would prefer to be soft and flexible, like a willow tree, rather than strong yet breakable, like an oak tree.

7. The classroom full of children hid behind their desks so <u>the children</u> could surprise their teacher.

8. Manny and I quickly sensed that <u>Manny and I</u> were not welcome in our new neighborhood.

9. The small sailboats in the regatta were not prepared for the storm, but <u>the boats</u> all made it back to the harbor safely.

10. After being sworn in as president, Lyndon B. Johnson promised that <u>Lyndon B. Johnson</u> would carry out John F. Kennedy's civil rights agenda.

34.2 Using objective case pronouns

Most of the following sentences contain underlined pronouns used incorrectly. Revise the incorrect sentences so that they contain correct objective case pronouns. If a sentence is correct, write C. (See *The Everyday Writer*, section 34a.) Example:

> me
> Eventually, the headwaiter told Kim, Stanley, and I̶ that we could be
>   ^
> seated.

1. Who do you think is the better tennis player, Mac or <u>he</u>?

2. The president gave <u>her</u> the highest praise.

3. The children wondered which presents under the tree were for <u>themselves</u>.

4. When we asked, the seller promised <u>we</u> that the software would work on our computer.

5. Though even the idea of hang gliding made <u>herself</u> nervous, she gave it a try.

6. The teacher praised <u>they</u> for asking thoughtful questions.

7. Cycling thirty miles a day was triathlon training for Bill, Ubijo, and <u>I</u>.

8. Dennis asked her and <u>me</u> to speak to him in the office.

9. Between you and <u>I</u>, that essay doesn't deserve a high grade.

10. I couldn't tell who was more to blame for the accident, <u>yourself</u> or Susan.

34.3 Using possessive case pronouns

Insert a possessive pronoun in the blank in each sentence. (See *The Everyday Writer*, section 34a.) Example:

> _____My____ **girlfriend bought flowers for me on Valentine's Day.**

1. All day long, people in the office asked admiringly, "_____

   flowers are those?"

2. I told them the bouquet was _____ .

3. The arrangement was perfectly complemented by _____

   vase, which my girlfriend had chosen.

4. _____ selection for me was red roses.

5. Every flower has _____ own meaning, according to a

   Victorian tradition.

6. Roses are easy to understand; _____ meaning is "true love."

7. My girlfriend knows that roses are my favorite flower;

   _____ are daffodils.

8. I really appreciated _____ going to the trouble and expense

   of buying me flowers.

9. Not only was it Valentine's Day, but she and I were also celebrating the

   anniversary of _____ first date.

10. That's the story of my most romantic moment; now tell me

    _____ .

34.4 Using *who, whoever, whom,* or *whomever*

Insert *who, whoever, whom,* or *whomever* appropriately in the blank
in each of the following sentences. (See *The Everyday Writer,* section
34b.) Example:

She is someone _____ *who* _____ **will go far.**

1. Professor Quinones asked _____ we wanted to collaborate

   with.

2. I would appreciate it if _____ made the mess in the kitchen could clean it up.

3. _____ shall I say is calling?

4. Soap operas appeal to _____ is interested in intrigue, suspense, joy, pain, grief, romance, fidelity, sex, and violence.

5. I have no sympathy for _____ was caught driving while intoxicated after the party Friday night.

6. _____ will the new tax law benefit most?

7. The plumbers _____ the landlord hired to install the new toilets in the building have botched the job.

8. She trusted only those _____ were members of her own family.

9. _____ did you think deserved the award?

10. The ballroom is available for children's parties or for _____ wants to rent it.

34.5 **Using pronouns in compound structures, appositives, elliptical clauses; choosing between *we* and *us* before a noun**

Choose the appropriate pronoun from the pair in parentheses in each of the following sentences. (See *The Everyday Writer,* sections 34c–e.) Example:

Of the group, only (<u>she</u>/her) and I finished the race.

1. All the other job applicants were far more experienced than (I/me).

2. Only (he/him) and the two dressmakers knew what his top-secret fall line would be like.

3. When Jessica and (she/her) first met, they despised each other.

4. I know that I will never again love anybody as much as (he/him).

5. To (we/us) New Englanders, hurricanes are a bigger worry than tornadoes.

6. The post-holiday credit card bills were a rude shock to Gary and (she/her).

7. Tomorrow (we/us) raw recruits will have our first on-the-job test.

8. When we heard the good news, we were happy for (they/them) and their children.

9. You may think that Anita will win Miss Congeniality, but in fact, everyone likes you better than (she/her).

10. Keith Richards scoffed at the words "Sir Mick Jagger," but (he/him) and Mick apparently don't agree about knighthood.

11. Just between you and (I/me), this seminar is a disaster!

12. Staying a week in a lakeside cabin gave (we/us) New Yorkers a much-needed vacation.

13. I always thought that my friend Alexis was the smartest of (we/us) all.

14. You might have studied harder than (I/me), but I still received a better grade.

15. Seeing (he and I/him and me) dressed up in her best clothes made Mom laugh until she saw the lipstick on the rug.

34.6 Maintaining pronoun-antecedent agreement

Revise the following sentences as needed to create pronoun-antecedent agreement and to eliminate the generic *he* and any awkward pronoun references. Some sentences can be revised in more than one way, and one sentence does not require any change. For the sentence that is correct as written, write C. (See *The Everyday Writer*, section 34f.) Example:

Almost everyone will encounter some type of allergy in their lifetime.

Most people will encounter some type of allergy in their lifetime.
OR
Almost everyone will encounter some type of allergy in his or her lifetime.

1. In general, neither dust mites nor pollen can cause life-threatening reactions, but it is among the most common allergens known.

2. A family that is prone to allergies may have a higher than usual percentage of allergic diseases, but their specific allergies are not necessarily the same for all family members.

3. If a person suspects that he might have an allergy, he can go to the doctor for a skin test or blood test.

4. Because of the severity and frequency of nut allergies in small children, a typical day-care center has rules specifying that they cannot allow any nut products.

5. Every meal and treat that is brought into the center must be screened to make sure their contents are nut free.

6. Even at the elementary school level, a class that shares a common snack may ask parents to avoid sending in nut products for their students.

7. In some cases, a school district's administration may decide to ban all nuts from their cafeterias.

8. Some feel that bans on nut products are intrusive, and they would prefer more lenient policies.

9. For people who are not allergic, almonds or a peanut butter sandwich can provide a healthy source of protein, so parents want to include them in their children's lunches.

10. One alternative idea to the total nut ban is the creation of "nut-free zones," where a child with an allergy can safely eat his food without any exposure to nuts.

34.7 Clarifying pronoun reference

Revise each of the following sentences to clarify pronoun reference. All the items can be revised in more than one way. If a pronoun refers ambiguously to more than one possible antecedent, revise the sentence to reflect each possible meaning. (See *The Everyday Writer,* section 34g.) Example:

After Jane left, Miranda found her keys.

Miranda found Jane's keys after Jane left.

Miranda found her own keys after Jane left.

1. Quint trusted Smith because she had worked for her before.

2. Not long after the company set up the subsidiary, it went bankrupt.

3. When drug therapy is combined with psychotherapy, the patients relate better to their therapists, are less vulnerable to what disturbs them, and are more responsive to them.

4. When Deyon was reunited with his father, he wept.

5. Bill smilingly announced his promotion to Ed.

6. On the weather forecast, it said to expect snow in the overnight hours.

7. The tragedy of child abuse is that even after the children of abusive parents grow up, they often continue the sad tradition of cruelty.

8. Lear divides his kingdom between the two older daughters, Goneril and Regan, whose extravagant professions of love are more flattering than the simple affection of the youngest daughter, Cordelia. The consequences of this error in judgment soon become apparent, as they prove neither grateful nor kind to him.

9. Anna smiled at her mother as she opened the birthday gift.

10. The visit to the pyramids was canceled because of the recent terrorist attacks on tourists there, which disappointed Kay, who had waited years to see them.

34.8 Revising to clarify pronoun reference

Revise the following paragraph to establish a clear antecedent for every pronoun that needs one. (See *The Everyday Writer,* section 34g.)

In Paul Fussell's essay "My War," he writes about his experience in combat during World War II, which he says still haunts his life. Fussell confesses that he joined the infantry ROTC in 1939 as a way of getting out of gym class, where he would have been forced to expose his "fat and flabby" body to the ridicule of his classmates. However, it proved to be a serious miscalculation. After the United States entered the war in 1941, other male college students were able to join officer training programs in specialized fields that kept them out of combat. If you were already in an ROTC unit associated with the infantry, though, you were trapped in it. That was how Fussell came to be shipped to France as a rifle-platoon leader in 1944. Almost immediately they sent him to the front, where he soon developed pneumonia because of insufficient winter clothing. He spent a month in hospitals; because he did not want to worry his parents, however, he told them it was just the flu. When he returned to the front, he was wounded by a shell that killed his sergeant.

35.1 Using adjectives and adverbs appropriately

Revise each of the following sentences to maintain correct adverb and adjective use. Then, for each adjective and adverb you've revised, point out the word that it modifies. (See *The Everyday Writer,* Chapter 35.) Example:

commonly

Almost every language ~~common~~ uses nonverbal cues that people can
interpret.

1. Most people understand easy that raised eyebrows indicate surprise.

2. When a man defiant crosses his arms across his chest, you probably
   do not need to ask what the gesture means.

3. You are sure familiar with the idea that bodily motions are a kind of
   language, but is the same thing true of nonverbal sounds?

4. If you feel sadly, your friends may express sympathy by saying,
   "Awww."

5. When food tastes well, diners express their satisfaction by murmuring,
   "Mmmm!"

6. If you feel relievedly that a long day is finally over, you may say,
   "Whew!"

7. These nonverbal signals are called "paralanguage," and they are
   quick becoming an important field of linguistic study.

8. Paralanguage "words" may look oddly on paper.

9. Written words can only partial indicate what paralanguage
   sounds like.

10. Lucky for linguists today, tape recorders are readily available.

35.2   Using comparative and superlative modifiers appropriately

Revise each of the following sentences to use modifiers correctly,
clearly, and effectively. A variety of acceptable answers is possible for
each sentence. (See *The Everyday Writer*, section 35c.) Example:

When Macbeth and Lady Macbeth plot to kill the king, she shows herself to be the ~~most~~ ^{more} ambitious of the two.
^

1. Some critics consider *Hamlet* to be Shakespeare's most finest tragedy.

2. Romeo and Juliet are probably the famousest lovers in all of literature.

3. The professor who acted out the hero's lines had the most unique teaching style.

4. Did you like the movie *Titus* or the play *Titus Andronicus* best?

5. One of my earlier memories is of seeing my mother onstage.

6. The star of the film is handsome, but he is the worse actor I have ever
   seen.

7. Shylock is not a likeable character, but he gives a more better speech
   than anyone else in the play.

8. The film was funny, but I like sad stories more.

9. My classmates and I disagree on which play made a better film: *King
   Lear, Macbeth,* or *Richard III.*

10. Shakespeare supposedly knew little Latin, but most people today know
    even littler.

36.1 Revising sentences with misplaced modifiers

Revise each of the following sentences by moving any misplaced modifiers so that they clearly modify the words they are intended to. You
may have to change grammatical structures for some sentences. (See
The Everyday Writer, section 36a.) Example:

Elderly people and students live in the neighborhood
surrounding the university/. ^{full of identical tract houses} ~~which is full of identical tract houses.~~
^   ^

1. Doctors recommend a new test for cancer, which is painless.

2. The tenor captivated the entire audience singing with verve.

3. I went through the process of taxiing and taking off in my mind.

4. The city approximately spent twelve million dollars on the new stadium.

5. Am I the only person who cares about modifiers in sentences that are misplaced?

6. On the day in question, the patient was not normally able to breathe.

7. Refusing to die at the end of the play, the audience stared in amazement at the actor playing Hamlet.

8. The clothes were full of holes that I was giving away.

9. Revolving out of control, the maintenance worker shut down the turbine.

10. A wailing baby was quickly kissed by the candidate with a soggy diaper.

36.2 Revising squinting modifiers, disruptive modifiers, and split infinitives

Revise each of the following sentences by moving disruptive modifiers and split infinitives as well as by repositioning any squinting modifier so that it unambiguously modifies either the word(s) before it or the word(s) after it. You may have to add words to a sentence to revise it adequately. (See *The Everyday Writer*, sections 36a and b.) Example:

The course we hoped would engross us completely bored us.

The course we hoped would completely engross us bored us.
OR
The course we hoped would engross us bored us completely.

1. Airline security personnel asked Ishmael, while he was hurrying to make his connecting flight, to remove his shoes and socks and to open his carry-on bag.

2. He remembered vividly enjoying the sound of Mrs. McIntosh's singing.

3. Bookstores sold, in the first week after publication, fifty thousand copies.

4. The mayor promised after her reelection she would not raise taxes.

5. The exhibit, because of extensive publicity, attracted large audiences.

6. The collector who owned the painting originally planned to leave it to a museum.

7. Doug hoped to perhaps this time succeed in training the cat to stay in one place even when it was not sleeping.

8. Doctors can now restore limbs that have been severed partially to a functioning condition.

9. A new housing development has gone up with six enormous homes on the hill across the road from Mr. Jacoby's farm.

10. The speaker said when he finished he would answer questions.

11. People who swim frequently will improve their physical condition.

12. The compost smelled after a long summer under the blazing sun pretty bad when I turned it.

13. The state commission promised at its final meeting to make its recommendations public.

14. Stella did not want to argue, after a long day at work and an evening class, about who was going to do the dishes.

15. In the next several months, Lynn hopes to despite her busy schedule of entertaining maintain her diet and actually lose weight.

36.3 Revising dangling modifiers

Revise each of the following sentences to correct the dangling modifiers. (See *The Everyday Writer*, section 36c.) Example:

a viewer gets
Watching television news, an impression is given of constant disaster.
^

1. High ratings are pursued by emphasizing fires and murders.

2. Interviewing grieving relatives, no consideration is shown for their privacy.

3. To provide comic relief, heat waves and blizzards are attributed to the weather forecaster.

4. Chosen for their looks, the newscasters' journalistic credentials are often weak.

5. As a visual medium, complex issues are hard to present in a televised format.

6. Assumed to care about no one except Americans, editorial boards for network news shows reject many international stories.

7. Generally only twenty-two minutes long, not including commercials, viewers have little time to absorb information.

8. Horrified by stories of bloodshed, the low probability of becoming the victim of crime or terrorism goes unrecognized.

9. Increasing fears among viewers, Americans worry about unlikely events such as children being kidnapped by strangers.

10. Not covering less sensational but more common dangers such as reckless driving and diabetes, viewers may not understand what is really likely to hurt them.

37.1 Revising comma splices and fused sentences

Revise each of the following comma splices or fused sentences by using the method suggested in brackets after the sentence. (See *The Everyday Writer*, Chapter 37.) Example:

, but
Americans think of slavery as a problem of the past it still exists
^
in some parts of the world. [Join with a comma and a coordinating conjunction.]

1. We tend to think of slavery only in U.S. terms in fact, it began long before the United States existed and still goes on. [Separate into two sentences.]

2. The group Human Rights Watch filed a report on Mauritania, it is a nation in northwest Africa. [Recast as one independent clause.]

3. Slavery has existed in Mauritania for centuries it continues today. [Join with a comma and a coordinating conjunction.]

4. Members of Mauritania's ruling group are called the Beydanes, they are an Arab Berber tribe also known as the White Moors. [Recast as one independent clause.]

5. Another group in Mauritania is known as the Haratin or the Black Moors, they are native West Africans. [Separate into two sentences.]

6. In modern-day Mauritania many of the Haratin are still slaves, they serve the Beydanes. [Join with a semicolon.]

7. The first modern outcry against slavery in Mauritania arose in 1980, protesters objected to the public sale of an enslaved woman. [Recast as an independent and a dependent clause.]

8. Mauritania outlawed slavery in 1981 little has been done to enforce the law. [Join with a comma and a coordinating conjunction.]

9. The law promised slaveholders financial compensation for freeing their slaves however, the language of the law did not explain exactly who would come up with the money. [Join with a semicolon.]

10. Physical force is not usually used to enslave the Haratin, rather, they are held by the force of conditioning. [Separate into two sentences.]

11. In some ways the Mauritanian system is different from slavery in the United States, there are few slave rebellions in Mauritania. [Join with a comma and a coordinating conjunction.]

12. By some estimates 300,000 former slaves still serve their old masters these slaves are psychologically and economically dependent. [Recast as an independent and a dependent clause.]

13. Many Mauritanian slaves live in their own houses, they may work for their former masters in exchange for a home or for food or medical care. [Recast as an independent and a dependent clause.]

14. In addition, there may be as many as 90,000 Haratin still enslaved, some Beydanes have refused to free their slaves unless the government pays compensation. [Join with a semicolon.]

15. Some Mauritanians claim that slavery is not a problem in their country in fact, in 2001, a Mauritanian official told a United Nations committee that slavery had never existed there. [Join with a dash.]

16. Of course, slavery must have existed in Mauritania there would have been no compelling reason to make a decree to abolish it in 1981. [Join with a comma and a coordinating conjunction.]

17. The president of Mauritania insisted in 1997 that discussions of modern slavery were intended only to hurt the country's reputation his comments did not offer much hope for opponents of slavery. [Recast as an independent and a dependent clause.]

18. Both the slaveholding Beydanes and the enslaved Haratin are made up largely of Muslims, some people in Mauritania see resistance to slavery in their country as anti-Muslim. [Join with a comma and a coordinating conjunction.]

19. In some cases, Western opponents of Mauritanian slavery may indeed harbor anti-Muslim sentiments that does not justify allowing the slavery to continue. [Join with a semicolon.]

20. Islamic authorities in Mauritania have agreed that all Muslims are equal therefore, one Muslim must not enslave another. [Join with a semicolon.]

37.2 Revising comma splices

Revise the following paragraph, eliminating all comma splices by using a period or a semicolon. Then revise the paragraph again, this time using any of these three methods:

Separate independent clauses into sentences of their own.

Recast two or more clauses as one independent clause.

Recast one independent clause as a dependent clause.

Comment on the two revisions. What differences in rhythm do you detect? Which version do you prefer, and why? (See *The Everyday Writer*, Chapter 37.)

My sister Julie is planning a spring wedding, obviously she is very excited. At first, she hoped for a simple affair, in fact, she wanted to elope with her fiancé, Mike. My mother was not happy about that, neither was Mike's mother. Julie agreed to a small party, however, it soon began to grow and grow. Julie decided to invite all her college roommates, also Mike wanted his boss and her husband to attend. The simple arrangement of roses she picked out quickly became an elaborate bundle of rare orchids, the DJ somehow turned into a full live band. The intimate restaurant she first chose could not hold all the guests, now she had to find a new venue. Julie and Mike were growing increasingly anxious, at the same time they were reluctant to disappoint their families. They finally decided on a small ceremony in the backyard for family members only, then a gigantic party afterward for family, friends, and co-workers. I can't wait to see my sister on the special day, she is going to be a beautiful and happy bride!

37.3 Revising comma splices and fused sentences

Revise the following paragraph, eliminating the comma splices and fused sentences by using any of these methods:

Separate independent clauses into sentences of their own.

Link clauses with a comma and a coordinating conjunction.

Link clauses with a semicolon and, perhaps, a conjunctive adverb or a transitional phrase.

Recast two or more clauses as one independent clause.

Recast one independent clause as a dependent clause.

Link clauses with a dash.

Then revise the paragraph again, this time eliminating each comma splice and fused sentence by using a different method. Decide which paragraph is more effective, and why. Finally, compare the revision you prefer with the revisions of several other students, and discuss the ways in which the versions differ in meaning. (See *The Everyday Writer*, Chapter 37.)

When I was a kid, the tooth fairy gave me fifty cents per tooth, now I see kids getting three dollars or more for each lost tooth! Some people think this "tooth inflation" is the symptom of something larger going on in our society, they think it may be that parents are trying to buy their way out of a guilty conscience. For example, parents feel bad about not spending enough time with their children, they may overcompensate in other areas, they may pay extra for a lost tooth. Problems can arise when children compare notes with other children they find out that the tooth fairy has been better to some families than others. Children may wonder why their teeth aren't worth as much as their friends', they may even wonder if they are being punished for something. In these cases, parents can help their children understand the situation better, for example they can explain that, as with other holidays and birthdays, everyone does not always receive identical gifts. Moreover, parents who find they are giving out more than the normal tooth fairy amount (around three dollars per tooth in 2012) may want to think about the message they are sending to their kids, it might not be the right one. For example, they may not want to keep the tooth fairy focused on money, instead they may want to create a handmade card or another special but inexpensive treat that the child will appreciate. In addition, parents may want to find ways to spend more time with their children, they may also want to teach the value of money by giving kids a regular allowance and assigning household chores in return. Eventually all kids will realize that their parents are acting as the tooth fairy, it is best if the message being sent teaches love and respect rather than greed and guilt.

38.1 Eliminating sentence fragments

Revise each of the following fragments, either by combining fragments with independent clauses or by rewriting them as separate sentences. (See *The Everyday Writer*, Chapter 38.) Example:

> **Zoe looked close to tears. Standing with her head bowed.**
>
> Standing with her head bowed, Zoe looked close to tears.
>
> Zoe looked close to tears. She was standing with her head bowed.

1. Autumn is a season of lavish bounty and stunning natural beauty. A season of giving thanks.

2. September is the perfect time to run outdoors. Avoiding the need to wait for a treadmill at a crowded gym.

3. To carve pumpkins and see scary movies. What better month than October?

4. For new college students who live on campus, the Columbus Day weekend often marks the first visit back home. For others, Thanksgiving. In any case, the event is often emotionally charged for both parents and students alike.

5. We decided to go camping one weekend in October. Pitching tents and setting up camp.

6. I can't tell if he is skipping the Halloween party because he is genuinely ill. Or if he just doesn't have an idea for a costume.

7. Turning the clocks back one hour in November. In theory, this makes better use of daylight.

8. My sister and her husband are hosting Thanksgiving dinner at their house this year. With Christmas at my parents' house and New Year's Eve at my cousin's. It should be a busy holiday season!

9. Your dreamy stuffing with cornbread, sausage, and sage. Please share the recipe with me!

10. Autumn often begins with hot, summerlike weather. Sometimes warm enough to go swimming outdoors! And by the end of the season, people are shoveling out their driveways and replacing flip-flops with snow boots.

38.2 Revising a paragraph to eliminate sentence fragments

Underline every fragment you find in the following paragraph. Then revise the paragraph. You may combine or rearrange sentences as long as you retain the original content. (See *The Everyday Writer*, Chapter 38.)

To study abroad or not. That is a major decision for many college students. Some will consider domestic programs at universities across the country. Traditionally, approaching their junior year. Opportunities for study in major cities and in small villages. Programs to satisfy every interest and major. While some are reluctant to leave behind the familiar comforts of college life, others look forward. To untold adventure and newfound freedom in exciting new environments. There's a lot to think about. Applications, courses, airfare, accommodations, and visas. Even though students yearn for the experience of studying abroad. Or outside their home university. Those who accept the challenge are generally rewarded. With a once-in-a-lifetime opportunity. Students who travel to foreign destinations can thoroughly immerse themselves in the culture, language, traditions and foods of their host country. And end up with new friends, an enhanced résumé, and a sense of self-reliance. Why not check with your college today? To see what kinds of foreign and domestic study programs you might apply to.

38.3 Understanding intentional fragments

Choose an advertisement that contains intentional fragments from a newspaper or magazine. Rewrite the advertisement to eliminate all sentence fragments. Be prepared to explain how your version and the original differ in impact and why you think the copywriters for the ad chose to use fragments rather than complete sentences. (See *The Everyday Writer*, Chapter 38.)

Punctuation and Mechanics

39.1 Using a comma to set off introductory elements

In the following sentences, add any commas that are needed after the introductory element. (See *The Everyday Writer*, section 39a.) Example:

> The inventor of pasteurization, Louis Pasteur was born in France in
> ^
> 1822.

1. Named after its inventor pasteurization is the process of heating liquids in order to destroy viruses and harmful bacteria.

2. Unlike sterilization pasteurization does not destroy all the pathogens in a food.

3. Instead pasteurization tries to reduce the number of all living organisms so they cannot cause illness.

4. While there are many methods of pasteurization the most commonly used is called HTST (for High Temperature/Short Time).

5. Although there are many foods and beverages that are pasteurized we generally think of the process in relation to dairy products.

6. Concerned about the helpful bacteria killed in the pasteurization process some people recommend drinking raw milk.

7. In addition raw milk advocates feel that modern cow breeds consume far too many antibiotics.

8. In stark contrast to their "mainstream" counterparts cows on raw milk dairy farms are not fed commercial feed.

9. Disturbed by the growing popularity of raw milk as a health food some doctors are speaking out in favor of mandatory pasteurization regulations.

10. Whatever your opinion on this issue it is unlikely that the debate will be settled soon.

39.2 Using a comma in compound sentences

Use a comma and a coordinating conjunction (*and, but, or, for, nor, so,* or *yet*) to combine each of the following pairs of sentences into one sentence. Delete or rearrange words if necessary. (See *The Everyday Writer,* section 39b.) Example:

> **There is a lot of talk these days about computer viruses, ~~Many~~ people do not know what they really are.** *, yet many*

1. Computer viruses are software programs. They are created to spread from one computer to another.

2. A biological virus cannot replicate itself. A virus must inject its DNA into a cell in order to reproduce.

3. Similarly, a computer virus must hitch on to some other computer program. Then it can launch itself.

4. These viruses can be totally destructive or basically benign. When people think of computer viruses, they generally think of the former.

5. Most viruses spread easily via attachments or instant messaging. One should never open an email attachment unless he or she knows the sender.

6. Viruses can be distributed through downloads. They can be spread through black-market software.

7. Computer users should not forget about installing a firewall to protect themselves. They should not ignore their computer's prompts to update security.

8. Children love to download computer games from sites they might be unfamiliar with. Parents and teachers should teach children about computer security.

9. Computer security protects the computer. It also protects the children.

10. The world of computer viruses might seem daunting. By following a few basic safety rules, computer users can largely protect themselves.

39.3 Recognizing restrictive and nonrestrictive elements

First, underline the restrictive or nonrestrictive elements in the following sentences. Then, use commas to set off the nonrestrictive elements in any of the sentences that contain such elements. (See *The Everyday Writer,* section 39c.) Example:

> *A Tale of Two Cities* **, <u>one of Charles Dickens's most famous works</u> ,**
> **was first published in 1859.**

1. The Hundred Years War which was actually a century-long series of conflicts was fought primarily between England and France.

2. Everyone who runs in the race will get a T-shirt and a small backpack.

3. Pablo Picasso, who lived to be ninety-one years old, is known for painting in several distinctly different styles throughout his life.

4. Mammals that have pouches to protect their young are known as marsupials.

5. Wasabi, a root that is related to horseradish, originated in Japan.

6. Plagiarism does occur on college campuses, even though it is dishonest and illegal.

7. The game will go into overtime if neither team scores within the next two minutes.

8. The downtown shopping area, hit hard during the recent financial crisis, is beginning to make a comeback.

9. Some people find that cilantro, an herb similar to parsley, tastes like soap.

10. We ordered seven pizzas, but the one with anchovies was left untouched.

11. My sports watch, which has more functions than I could ever use, is surprisingly not waterproof.

12. The boy, red-faced and completely out of breath, collapsed into his father's arms.

13. A phone call in the middle of the night can be very upsetting.

14. Any student who wishes to complete an independent study must find a professor to act as sponsor.

15. The New Orleans Jazz and Heritage Festival, an annual celebration of food, dance, and music, takes place every spring.

39.4 Using commas to set off items in a series

In the following sentences, add any commas that are needed to set off words, phrases, or clauses in a series. If no comma is needed, write C. (See *The Everyday Writer*, section 39d.) Example:

The waiter brought water, menus, and an attitude.

1. I am very excited to see Alcatraz visit Chinatown and tour Napa Valley.

2. I am looking forward to turning eighteen being able to vote and perhaps serving in the military.

3. The spider's orange body resembles a colored dot amidst eight long black legs.

4. The moon circles the earth the earth revolves around the sun and the sun is just one star among many in the Milky Way galaxy.

5. The ball sailed over the fence across the road and through the Wilsons' window.

6. He is a brilliant demanding renowned concert pianist.

7. They found employment in truck driving farming and mining.

8. My top three favorite nineties bands are Pearl Jam Nirvana and Soundgarden, in that order.

9. Joan is a skilled human resource manager.

10. Superficial observation does not provide accurate insight into people's lives—how they feel what they believe in how they respond to others.

39.5   Using commas to set off parenthetical and transitional expressions, contrasting elements, interjections, direct address, and tag questions

Revise each of the following sentences, using commas to set off parenthetical and transitional expressions, contrasting elements, interjections, words used in direct address, and tag questions. (See *The Everyday Writer,* sections 39e and f.) Example:

Ladies and gentlemen, thank you for your attention.
                              ^

1. Ouch that tetanus shot really hurt!

2. Doctor Ross you are over an hour late for our appointment.

3. Consider furthermore the impact of environmental destruction on future generations.

4. The West in fact has become solidly Republican in presidential elections.

5. Last year I am sorry to say six elms had to be destroyed.

6. Captain Kirk I'm a doctor not a madman.

7. The celebration will alas conclude all too soon.

8. One must consider the society as a whole not just its parts.

9. You didn't really think I would fall for that trick did you?

10. Mary announced, "Kids I want you to clean your rooms not make a bigger mess."

39.6 Using commas with dates, addresses, titles, numbers, and quotations

Revise each of the following sentences, using commas appropriately with dates, addresses and place-names, titles, numbers, and quotations. If no comma is needed in a sentence, write C. (See *The Everyday Writer*, sections 39g and h.) Example:

The wine store's original location was 2373 Broadway, New York City.
                                                                      ^

1. "Education is not the filling of a pail, but the lighting of a fire" said William Butler Yeats.

2. I agree with Groucho Marx that "humor is reason gone mad."

3. "The public be damned!" William Henry Vanderbilt was reported to have said. "I'm working for my stockholders."

4. "Who can match the desperate humorlessness of the adolescent who thinks he is the first to discover seriousness?", asks P. J. Kavanaugh.

5. 1600 Pennsylvania Avenue Washington DC is a familiar address to many.

6. On July 21 1969 Neil Armstrong became the first person to walk on the moon.

7. On the tomb, under the name *Rev. Martin Luther King Jr.*, is a quotation from a famous speech: "Free at last, free at last, thank God almighty I'm free at last."

8. "Neat people are lazier and meaner than sloppy people" according to Suzanne Britt.

9. Ithaca New York has a population of about 30000.

10. In my dictionary, the rules of punctuation begin on page 1560.

39.7 Eliminating unnecessary commas

Revise each of the following sentences, deleting unnecessary commas. If a sentence contains no unnecessary commas, write *C*. (See *The Everyday Writer*, section 39j.) Example:

Insomniacs are people/who have a hard time sleeping soundly.

1. Contrary to popular belief, insomnia is not simply a matter, of being unable to sleep well at night.

2. Insomniacs do indeed wake up at night, but, studies have demonstrated that they also have trouble napping during the day.

3. Why can't insomniacs sleep soundly at night, or nap when they are tired?

4. In many cases, insomniacs suffer, from anxiety.

5. Doctors and sleep researchers, have long considered anxiety to be a common result of getting too little sleep.

6. However, recent studies indicate that anxiety contributes to sleeplessness, not the other way around.

7. Therapies to help insomniacs, include behavior modification and sleeping pills.

8. Sleep therapists recommend, going to bed at the same time every night, not watching television in bed, and not reading in bed.

9. Restless, disturbed, sleep habits are certainly irritating, but are they also, bad for an insomniac's health?

10. While tired people are more dangerous drivers, and less productive workers, no one knows for certain, if insomnia can actually make them sick.

40.1 Using semicolons to link clauses

Combine each of the following pairs of sentences into one sentence by using a semicolon. (See *The Everyday Writer*, section 40a.) Example:

I decided to start my diet this week/ Not surprisingly, a package just
arrived from my mother with brownies, cookies, and three different
flavors of popcorn.

(handwritten: ; not)

1. This sofa is much too big. It will never fit inside my Prius.

2. The business could no longer afford to pay its bills or its employees. Therefore, the owners filed for bankruptcy.

3. German shepherds are known for their intelligence. They are also known for their protective behavior.

4. Once they live off campus, most students begin cooking their own meals. Nevertheless, some choose to maintain their school dining plans.

5. Natalia ran a marathon in four hours and two minutes. Unfortunately, this time did not qualify her for the Boston Marathon.

6. The largest land animal is the African elephant. Indeed, typical males reach twenty feet in length and weigh over 16,500 pounds.

7. America is full of surprising roadside attractions. One of the most notable is the Corn Palace in Mitchell, South Dakota.

8. This expert trail is steep, narrow, and bumpy. Only advanced skiers should attempt to go down it.

9. This internship is nearby, in my field of study, and has great hours. However, it doesn't pay any money.

10. Our senator continues to support tax cuts for the wealthiest Americans. Meanwhile, millions remain unemployed.

40.2   Revising misused semicolons

Revise each of the following sentences to correct the misuse of semicolons. If the semicolon in a sentence is appropriate as written, write C. (See *The Everyday Writer*, section 40c.) Example:

The new system would encourage high school students to take more academic courses͟ͅ thus strengthening college preparation.

1. To make the tacos, I need to buy; ground beef, beans, and tortillas.

2. Verbal scores have decreased by more than fifty-four points; while math scores have decreased by more than thirty-six.

3. For four glorious but underpaid weeks; I'll be working in Yosemite this summer.

4. Finally, I found her at the Humane Society; a beautiful shepherd-collie mix who likes children and plays well with cats.

5. If the North had followed up its victory at Gettysburg more vigorously; the Civil War might have ended sooner.

6. He enjoys commuting to work on the train; although it can get crowded at rush hour.

7. Some gardeners want; low-maintenance plants, limited grass to mow, and low water usage.

8. She dozed off through most of her art history lectures; as a result, she is in danger of failing the course.

9. After school; many fourteen-year-olds head to the mall; where they spend the rest of the day.

10. I will meet you at the movies; as soon as I finish writing my term paper.

41.1 Using periods appropriately

Revise each of the following items, inserting periods in the appropriate places and eliminating any inappropriate punctuation. If a sentence is correct as written, write C. (See *The Everyday Writer*, section 41a.) Example:

> **Over the centuries, some of history's most interesting characters have**
>
> **been women/.**
>   ^

1. Cleopatra, the last ruler of ancient Egypt, was known for her ability to gain the support of powerful men in order to solidify her own role as leader

2. When her army was defeated by the Romans in 30 BCE and her husband Marc Antony killed himself, some say she committed suicide by means of an asp bite?

3. In China, the brief reign of Empress Wu from 690 to 705 CE saw some changes that benefited women

4. The empress commissioned the biographies of famous women, decreed that the mourning period for mothers be made equal to that of fathers, and mandated the creation of a character for "human being" that depicted life flowing from a single woman!

5. In 1903, Polish physicist and chemist Marie Curie was the first woman ever to receive a Nobel Prize.

6. Ms Curie discovered two new elements—radium and polonium—and pioneered the understanding of radioactivity.

7. A woman named Jane Addams, appalled at the corruption she saw in city government, became active in helping poor residents of Chicago and eventually helped shape public policy in Washington, DC

8. Around 1900, Ms Addams got herself appointed garbage inspector and rode atop the garbage wagon every morning at 6:00 AM so that she could personally ensure that garbage was being collected in poor districts as well as rich.

9. In 1893, a young woman named Alice Hamilton earned her MD and went on to become a toxicology specialist, working to protect employees in industrial jobs from harmful substances

10. In 1919, Dr Hamilton, who lived to be 101 years old, was the first woman ever hired as a professor at Harvard University.

41.2 Using question marks appropriately

Revise each of the following sentences, adding question marks, substituting question marks for other punctuation where appropriate, and removing inappropriately placed question marks. Some sentences do not require any question marks; for those sentences, write C. (See *The Everyday Writer,* section 41b.) Example:

She asked the travel agent, "What is the air fare to Greece?"

1. I couldn't tell if she was offended by my remarks or amused by them?

2. "Which Harry Potter book did you like best," Georgia asked Harriet?

3. I couldn't stop thinking about my choices after graduation: should I get an entry-level job at a Fortune 500 company. Go to law school. Teach English at an inner-city high school?

4. "Who wants to go to the pool with me" asked May?

5. Liam asked his mother if he could go with his friends to the concert?

6. She wondered if he would ever call back.

7. Do you remember who said, "Be the change you want to see in the world?"

8. We began to ask what might fix the problem—restarting the computer, closing other programs, using a different browser.

9. Is your favorite Springsteen song "Atlantic City"?

10. I asked her if she would be much longer in the bathroom?

41.3 Using exclamation points appropriately

Revise each of the following sentences, adding or deleting exclamation points as necessary and removing any other inappropriate punctuation that you find. (See *The Everyday Writer,* section 41c.) Example:

> ! The
> **Look out/~~the~~ tide is coming in fast/** !

1. The defendant stood up in the witness box and shouted, "I didn't do it. You've got to believe me."

2. Oh, no. We've lost the house.

3. The child cried, "Ouch" as her mother pulled off the bandage!

4. "Go! Go! Go!," roared the crowd as the quarterback sped toward the end zone.

5. What, exactly, do you want!?

6. It was an ordinary school day, so the child once again came home to an empty house!

7. Stop, thief.

8. She exclaimed, "It's too hot."

9. The only thing the surprised guest of honor could say was, "Well, I'll be!".

10. "This is ridiculous," sputtered the diner as the waiter brought the wrong

    order again!

42.1 Using apostrophes to signal possession

Complete each of the following sentences by inserting 's or an apostrophe alone to form the possessive case of the italicized words. (See *The Everyday Writer,* section 42a.) Example:

Many Internet scare stories are nothing but old *wives'* tales.

1. Internet rumors circulate widely because of *people* good intentions.

2. Recipients who pass on messages want everyone to hear about a *child* inspiring fight against cancer or about some dangerous drug, product, or disease.

3. The *Internet* power to inform is great, but so is its power to play tricks on unsuspecting people.

4. A *hoax* creators count on *recipients* kind hearts and concern for the well-being of their families and friends.

5. *Consumers* fears fuel some of the Internet medical scares.

6. Have you heard the one about how *deodorants* ingredients supposedly clog your pores and cause cancer?

7. Another scare warned that sugar substitutes caused the *body* immune system to malfunction.

8. Some of these scares are probably intended to damage certain *corporations* reputations by spreading rumors about products.

9. Others, like the one about checking your toilet seat to be sure it has not become a deadly *spider* hiding place, probably begin as jokes.

10. The *Internet* speed has made such anonymous rumors spread more rapidly than anyone would have thought possible twenty years ago.

42.2 Using apostrophes to create contractions

Revise each of the following sentences so that it uses contractions. Remove any misused apostrophes. (See *The Everyday Writer,* section 42b.) Example:

> I'll
> ~~I will~~ bring some meatballs to the potluck dinner.
> ^

1. Genevieve was not even three years old when she moved here from Germany, so she does not have a German accent.

2. You will see plenty of advertisements on television for alcoholic beverages, but you will not see any for tobacco products.

3. Whose dog is it that keeps scratching it's ears?

4. It has been almost ten years, but I cannot forget how I felt on the night we received the terrible news.

5. Let us go to the later movie, after he has had a chance to finish his homework.

6. Restaurants do not usually take personal checks, so I had better remember to get some cash before we go.

7. Who is the professor that he would like to have for economics next semester?

8. I am always up for a game of chess, but I would not want to play for money.

9. It has been said that a chain is only as strong as it's weakest link.

10. Dylan knew she would not mind if he was not able to attend her performance.

43.1 Using quotation marks to signal direct quotations

In the following sentences, add quotation marks each time someone else's exact words are being used. Some sentences do not require quotation marks; mark correct sentences C. (See *The Everyday Writer*, section 43a.) Example:

" "
Your phone's ringing! yelled Phil from the end of the hall.
^   ^

1. Dr. King was quoting an old African American spiritual when he said, Free at last! Free at last! Thank God Almighty, we are free at last.

2. My mother told us we had to get in the car immediately or she wouldn't drive us.

3. It's not fair, she told him. You always win.

4. To paraphrase his words, "the planet is in deep trouble if we don't start reducing carbon emissions."

5. Call me Ishmael is the first sentence of novelist Herman Melville's *Moby Dick.*

6. Most people like to think of themselves as open-minded and flexible enough to change when the circumstances demand.

7. After repeating I can't hear you with her fingers stuck in her ears, Hannah ran to her room and slammed the door.

8. I could not believe the condition of my hometown, he wrote.

9. Keep your opinions to yourselves, Dad muttered as he served the lumpy oatmeal.

10. Is the computer plugged in? the technical support operator asked, prompting Harry to snarl, Yes, I'm not a complete idiot.

43.2 Using quotation marks for titles and definitions

Revise each of the following sentences by using quotation marks appropriately to signal titles and definitions. (See *The Everyday Writer*, section 43c and d.) Example:

> **One of the best short stories we read last semester was**
> **"**   **"**
> **The Story of an Hour by Kate Chopin.**
> ^   ^

1. The term *mulatto*, which means a person of mixed black and white ancestry, is considered offensive to many and therefore should be avoided.

2. The Red Wheelbarrow is often considered to be William Carlos Williams's most important poem.

3. The Rolling Stones song Time Is on My Side was first recorded by Irma Thomas.

4. My favorite episode of *Glee* is Theatricality, especially since the cast performed the Lady Gaga song Poker Face.

5. The *New York Times* article Dealing with Student Debt helps college graduates understand the best way to handle their student loans.

6. After a long hiatus, *Mad Men* returned in March 2012 with a two-hour premiere called A Little Kiss.

7. In the essay Spin Right and Shoot Left, author John McPhee finds himself describing the rules of lacrosse to an Irish cab driver.

8. At the very end of the last Harry Potter book, in a chapter called The Prince's Tale, the author finally reveals the true nature of Harry's nemesis, Professor Severus Snape.

9. Sherwood Anderson's book *Winesburg, Ohio* is a collection of inter-twined short stories, including Hands, Respectability, and The Untold Lie.

10. I realized that all my vocabulary studying had paid off when I saw the word *ephemeral* and knew that it meant short-lived.

43.3 Using quotation marks appropriately

Revise each of the following sentences by adding necessary quotation marks, deleting or moving quotation marks used inappropriately, or changing wording as necessary. (See *The Everyday Writer,* Chapter 43.) Example:

> **Readers and filmgoers have once again been ˄"captivated˄" by vampire stories.**

1. Vampire legends date back hundreds of years, but the characters and plots are constantly being "reinvented."

2. The four-book series that began with the novel *Twilight* by Stephenie Meyer was an "enormous" success.

3. The film adaptations of the books have grossed over "$2 billion" worldwide.

4. The soundtrack for the first film in the series includes the hit single Decode by the band Paramore.

5. Much has been said about the series, both "good" and "bad."

6. Patty Campbell's editorial review on Amazon.com calls the first novel, *Twilight,* an "exquisite fantasy".

7. In the *Washington Post* article Love Bites, reviewer Elizabeth Hand criticizes Meyer's portrayal of the main character in the series, Bella Swan, as being passive and weak.

8. The *New York Times* review, by Elizabeth Spires, praises *Twilight*'s ability to depict "a fatal attraction to someone or something dangerously different", but says that the writing is at times "overearnest" and "amateurish."

9. Regardless of the criticism, both positive and negative, the *Twilight* series has been an "undisputed" commercial success, both in bookstores and at the box office.

10. Television shows such as *"The Vampire Diaries,"* have also benefited from a public fascination with the undead.

44.1 Using parentheses and brackets

Revise the following sentences, using parentheses and brackets correctly. Change any other punctuation in the sentences as needed. (See *The Everyday Writer*, sections 44a and b.) Example:

> **Since the disputed presidential election of 2000, many observers**
>
> **(and not just from right-wing media outlets) have argued that U.S.**
>
> **journalists are not doing a thorough job of presenting political issues.**

1. The words *media elite* have been said so often usually by people who are themselves elite members of the media that the phrase has taken on a life of its own.

2. Are the media really elite, and are they really liberal, as talk-show regulars (Ann Coulter, for example argue)?

3. Media critic Eric Alterman has coined the term "so-called liberal media" [SCLM] because he believes that the media have been intimidated by criticism.

4. An article in the *Journal of Communication* discussing the outcome of recent U.S. elections explained that "claiming the media are liberally biased perhaps has become a core rhetorical strategy" used by conservatives, qtd. in Alterman 14.

5. Some progressive groups (including Fairness and Accuracy in Reporting (FAIR)) keep track of media coverage of political issues and campaigns.

6. However, liberals are not the only media watchdogs: right-wing organizations, including Accuracy in Media, (AIM) also closely examine the way political stories are reported.

7. The nonpartisan Campaign Desk Web site [sponsored by the *Columbia Journalism Review*] was dedicated to tracking media coverage of the 2004 presidential election.

8. According to the site's home page, the purpose of Campaign Desk was "to straighten and deepen campaign coverage" as a resource for voters (most of whom rely on media coverage to make decisions about the candidates.)

9. Is truly objective coverage of hot-button issues and political candidates, (whether Republicans or Democrats,) ever possible?

10. And can we forget that as media consumers, we have an obligation to be an informed electorate (even though it's easy to pay attention only to the news that reinforces our own beliefs.)?

44.2 Using dashes

Revise the following sentences so that dashes are used correctly. If the sentence is correct as written, write *C*. (See *The Everyday Writer*, section 44c.) Example:

In some states California, for example banks are no longer allowed to charge ATM users an additional fee for withdrawing money.

1. Many consumers accept the fact that they have to pay additional fees for services like bank machines if they don't want to pay, they don't have to use the service.

2. Nevertheless,—extra charges seem to be added to more and more services all the time.

3. Some of the charges are ridiculous why should hotels charge guests a fee for making a toll-free telephone call?

4. The hidden costs of service fees are irritating people feel that their bank accounts are being nibbled to death.

5. But some of the fees consumers are asked to pay—are more than simply irritating.

6. The "convenience charges"—that people have to pay when buying show tickets by telephone—are often a substantial percentage of the cost of the ticket.

7. If ticket buyers don't want to pay these "convenience charges" and who does? they must buy their tickets at the box office.

8. Finally, there are government fees that telephone companies and other large corporations are required to pay.

9. Telephone companies routinely pass these fees used to ensure Internet access to remote areas and schools along to their customers, implying that the government expects consumers to pay.

10. Many consumers are not aware that the government requires the corporations—not the general public—to pay these fees.

44.3 Using colons

Insert a colon in each of the following sentences that needs one. Remove any misused colons. Some sentences do not require a colon; if the sentence is correct as written, write C. (See *The Everyday Writer*, section 44d.) Example:

I like most seafood except̸ salmon, oysters, and clams.

1. The reading at their wedding Mass was from 1 Corinthians 13, 4–7.

2. Ali, Ayaan Hirsi. *Infidel.* New York, Free Press, 2007.

3. On January 1, Emmit listed his New Year's resolutions, lose twenty pounds, start a retirement account, and cook a healthy meal once a week.

4. The ratio of boys to girls in that preschool is 3–1.

5. The emcee looked out at the crowd and dared us to make more noise "I can't hear you!"

6. I am considering several different careers, including marketing, public relations, and broadcasting.

7. All we could do was watch as the other boats reeled in fish after fish, bass, pike, trout, and perch.

8. Rose has trophies for several different sports: basketball, lacrosse, soft-ball, and soccer.

9. The 2011 film *Captain America The First Avenger* was both a critical and commercial success.

10. My roommate's annoying habits include: forgetting to lock the door, leaving dirty dishes in the sink, and playing loud video games late at night.

44.4 Using ellipses

Read the following passage. Then assume that the underlined portions have been left out in a reprinting of the passage. Indicate how you would use ellipses to indicate those deletions. (See *The Everyday Writer*, section 44f.) Example:

Saving money is difficult for young people in entry-level positions, but it is important.

Should young people <u>who are just getting started in their careers</u> think about saving for retirement? Those who begin to save in their twenties <u>are making a wise financial decision. They</u> are putting away money that can earn compound interest for decades. Even if they save only a hundred dollars a month, and even if they stop saving when they hit age thirty-five, the total forty years later will be impressive. <u>On the other hand,</u> people who wait until they are fifty to begin saving will have far less money put aside at the age of sixty-five. People who wait too long may face an impoverished retirement <u>unless they are able to save thousands of dollars each month.</u> Of course, no one knows how long he or she will live, but saving is a way of gambling on reaching retirement. Difficult as it may be to think about being sixty-five or seventy years old, young people should plan ahead.

44.5 Reviewing punctuation marks

Correct the punctuation in the following sentences. If the punctuation is already correct, write C. (See *The Everyday Writer,* Chapters 39–44.) Example:

> **Children/ who are too young to speak/ are often frustrated because they cannot communicate their wishes.**

1. Many American parents are willing to try almost anything prenatal music, infant flash cards, you name it to help their children succeed.

2. Some parental efforts do help children, for instance, children whose parents read to them are more likely to enjoy books.

3. Other schemes to make babies smarter, such as the so-called "Mozart effect," apparently don't make much difference.

4. A new idea that is "popular" with many parents of young children is sign language.

5. Researcher Joseph Garcia an expert in child development and in American Sign Language noticed that hearing babies with deaf parents often learned sign language before they could speak.

6. By sixteen to eighteen months, most children are able to speak simple words, and make themselves understood.

7. However, babies can communicate simple ideas to their parents starting at about eight months, if the infants learn signs.

8. Garcia showed that parents could easily teach their children signs for words like please, more, sleepy, and hungry.

9. Garcia wrote a book called "Sign with Your Baby."

10. Not surprisingly, parents bought the book, (and then the video,) and now sign-language classes for small children are easy to find.

11. Parents who go to signing classes with their infants and toddlers hope for a good outcome; better communication between parent and child and less frustration for both.

12. A study by California researchers found that seven-year-olds earned slightly higher IQ scores if they had learned to sign as infants.

13. It's not surprising that this studys results fueled the demand for more toddler sign-language classes.

14. The researchers who developed the study said that the best reason for parents to sign with their children was to allow the children "to communicate what they need and see".

15. One researcher, Dr Elizabeth Bates, told the "New York Times" that the hand movements that small children can learn are really gestures, not proper sign language.

16. Others contend that the childrens' hand movements stand for concepts so the movements are sign language.

17. Some parents fear that a child who learns to communicate by signs will have little incentive to speak researchers have found no evidence of this effect.

18. In fact children who can use sign language are often especially eager to learn how to speak.

19. While signing appears to have some benefits for the children who learn it not everyone feels that parents need to rush out to attend a class.

20. Any activity that gets parents to spend more time communicating with their children probably has it's benefits.

45.1 Capitalizing

Capitalize words as needed in the following sentences. (See *The Everyday Writer*, Chapter 45.) Example:

$\overset{T}{\cancel{t}}.\ \overset{S}{\cancel{s}}.\ \overset{E}{\cancel{e}}$liot, who wrote $\overset{T}{\cancel{t}}$he $\overset{W}{\cancel{w}}$aste $\overset{L}{\cancel{l}}$and, was an editor at $\overset{F}{\cancel{f}}$aber and $\overset{F}{\cancel{f}}$aber.

1. johnny depp appeared to be having a wonderful time playing captain jack sparrow in *pirates of the caribbean: the curse of the black pearl*.

2. the battle of lexington and concord was fought in april 1775.

3. i will cite the novels of vladimir nabokov, in particular *pnin* and *lolita*.

4. accepting an award for his score for the film *the high and the mighty*, dmitri tiomkin thanked beethoven, brahms, wagner, and strauss.

5. i wondered if my new levi's were faded enough.

6. We drove east over the hudson river on the tappan zee bridge.

7. senator trent lott was widely criticized after appearing to praise senator strom thurmond's segregationist past.

8. "bloody sunday" was a massacre of catholic protesters in derry, northern ireland, on january 30, 1972.

9. we had a choice of fast-food, chinese, or italian restaurants.

10. the town in the American south where i was raised had a statue of a civil war soldier in the center of main street.

46.1 Using abbreviations

Revise each of the following sentences to eliminate any abbreviations that would be inappropriate in academic writing. If a sentence is correct, write C. (See *The Everyday Writer*, sections 46a–g.) Example:

>   international
> The ~~intl.~~ sport of belt sander racing began in a hardware store.
>   ^

1. Nielson Hardware in Point Roberts, WA, was the site of the world's first belt sander race in 1989.

2. The power tools, ordinarily used for sanding wood, are placed on a thirty-ft. track and plugged in; the sander to reach the end first wins.

3. Today, the International Belt Sander Drag Race Association (IBSDRA) sponsors tours of winning sanders, an international championship, and a Web site that sells IBSDRA T-shirts.

4. There are three divisions of belt sander races: the stock div., which races sanders right out of the box; the modified div., which allows any motor the owner wants to add; and the decorative div., which provides a creative outlet for sander owners.

5. An average race lasts two seconds, but the world champion modified sander raced the track in 1.52 secs.

6. The fastest sanders run on very coarse sandpaper—a no. sixteen grit is an excellent choice if it's available.

7. Stock sanders are usually widely available brands, e.g., Mikita or Bosch.

8. The S-B Power Tool Co. in Chicago, maker of Bosch sanders, allows participants to race its tools, but the co. does not underwrite races.

9. Another tool company, the Do It Best Corp. of Wayne, Ind., sponsors races across the U.S. and Canada.

10. No one knows what % of the nation's power tools have been used for this kind of entertainment.

46.2 Spelling out numbers and using figures

Revise the numbers in the following sentences as necessary for correctness and consistency. If a sentence is correct, write *C*. (See *The Everyday Writer*, sections 46h–j.) Example:

> 365
> There are ~~three hundred sixty-five~~ days in a year, except for leap years,
>   ^   366
> which have ~~three hundred sixty-six~~ days.
>   ^

1. *The Simpsons* has been on the air for more than 23 seasons, making it the longest-running prime-time series ever in American television.

2. After 4 years of college, I expect to graduate on June ten, 2014.

3. The hotel is located at three-zero-one Dauphin Street, New Orleans, Louisiana.

4. The last time she checked, Kira had 3,457 friends on Facebook; I have only eighty-two, and I like it that way!

5. 248 new members joined the public radio station during this year's pledge drive, compared with just 92 new members last year.

6. In the United States, forty-three percent of mobile phones in use are smartphones.

7. An old vinyl record, or LP (for "long play"), would spin on the turntable at a rate of thirty-three and one-third rounds per minute.

8. The Tigers beat the Rangers by a score of 5–3.

9. The new bridge will cost $72 million over two years of construction.

10. The bus arrives every weekday at six fifty-eight AM.

47.1 Using italics

In each of the following sentences, underline any words that should be italicized, and circle any italicized words that should not be. If a title requires quotation marks instead of italicization, add them. (See *The Everyday Writer,* Chapter 47.) Example:

> The United States still abounds with regional speech — for example,
>
> many people in the Appalachians still use local words such as <u>crick</u>
>
> and <u>holler</u>.

1. *Regionalism,* a nineteenth-century literary movement, focused on the language and customs of people in areas of the country not yet affected by industrialization.

2. Regional writers produced some American classics, such as Mark Twain's Huckleberry Finn and James Fenimore Cooper's Last of the Mohicans.

3. Twain, not an admirer of Cooper's work, wrote a scathing essay about his predecessor called *The Literary Offenses of James Fenimore Cooper.*

4. Some of the most prolific regional writers were women like Kate Chopin, who wrote her first collection of short stories, Bayou Folk, to help support her family.

5. The stories in *Bayou Folk,* such as the famous *Désirée's Baby,* focus on the natives of rural Louisiana.

6. Chopin also departed from regional works to explore women's experiences of marriage, as in her short piece *The Story of an Hour.*

7. In Maine, Sarah Orne Jewett wrote sketches of rural life that appeared in the Atlantic Monthly.

8. She later turned these into a novel, Deephaven, which she hoped would "teach the world that country people were not . . . ignorant."

9. Her finest short story, *A White Heron,* and her celebrated novel *The Country of the Pointed Firs* also benefit from settings in Maine.

10. Many regional stories—Stephen Crane's *The Bride Comes to Yellow Sky* is a prime example—show the writer's concern that an isolated culture is in danger of disappearing.

48.1 Using hyphens in compounds and with prefixes

Insert hyphens as needed. A dictionary will help you with some items. If an item does not require a hyphen, write C. (See *The Everyday Writer,* Chapter 48.) Example:

full‐bodied wine

1. a thirty nine year old woman

2. my ex mother in law

3. singer songwriter Leslie Feist

4. devil may care attitude

5. mass produced goods

6. widely known poet

7. self righteous know it all

8. pro NAFTA crowd

9. ill gotten gains

10. one hundred and one Dalmatians

48.2   Using hyphens appropriately

Insert or delete hyphens as necessary in the following sentences. Use your dictionary if necessary. If a sentence is correct as printed, write C. (See *The Everyday Writer*, Chapter 48.) Example:

> The bleary eyed student finally (stop/)
>
> / ped fighting sleep and went to bed.

1. His write-up on the race captured the excitement perfectly.

2. The House Unamerican Activities Committee was formed in 1937.

3. Joe seemed like a very angry-young-man.

4. Remember to drop-off your medical forms.

5. Her vacation was much-needed.

6. Please remind Jane to pick-up the clothes from the dry cleaners.

7. It's hard to believe that 90 percent of the world's water is salty.

8. I have a nine-year-old daughter, and the younger one is nearly five-years-old.

9. My mother is an ex-smoker; she quit when the warning appeared on all packs of cigarettes.

10. The sign up sheet is outside the gymnasium.

For Multilingual Writers

Revise the following sentences or nonsentences so that they have explicit subjects and objects as necessary. If a sentence does not contain an error, write C. (See *The Everyday Writer,* section 57a.) Example:

It is
~~Is~~ easy and convenient for people with access to computers to shop
online.

1. No faster way to take care of holiday shopping.

2. Computers also allow people to buy items they cannot find locally.

3. Banks and credit-card companies have Web sites now, and consumers use for making payments, looking at statements, and transferring balances.

4. Are problems with doing everything online, of course.

5. Customers must use credit cards, and thieves want to break in and get.

6. Are small-time thieves and juvenile pranksters disrupting online services.

7. Jamming popular sites is one way for hackers to gain notoriety, and have been several such actions.

8. A hacker can get enormous amounts of online data, even if are supposed to be secure.

9. People have every right to be concerned about online privacy, for is a tremendous amount of private information stored in online databases, including medical records and financial data.

10. Internet users must use caution and common sense online, but is also essential for online information to be safeguarded by security experts.

57.2 Editing for English word order

Revise the following sentences as necessary. If a sentence does not contain an error, write C. (See *The Everyday Writer*, section 57b.) Example:

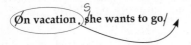

1. To sleep he wishes to go now.

2. He displays proudly in the window a flag.

3. Comes in first the runner from Kenya.

4. She should go not into the woods alone.

5. A passing grade she wants.

6. Extremely poorly Sandy drove during her first road test.

7. Slow and easy wins the race.

8. Desserts some restaurant guests would like to begin with.

9. John watches videos incessantly.

10. "Speak fluently English," ordered the instructor.

57.3 Using noun clauses, infinitives, and gerunds appropriately

Revise the following sentences as necessary so that each contains an appropriate noun clause, infinitive, or gerund positioned well. If a sentence does not contain an error, write C. (See *The Everyday Writer*, sections 57c and d.) Example:

> that
> **It pleases me you like me.**
> ^

1. Is important that we think in English.

2. We discussed to go to a movie, but we could not agree on what to see.

3. It annoys the teacher we don't practice conversation.

4. It is possible that you are right.

5. Ashok refused answering his sister's questions.

6. Her mother stopped to drive on her ninetieth birthday.

7. What he has to say is of great interest to me.

8. It is obvious that she made the right decision.

9. No one expected being allowed to leave work before midnight.

10. We appreciated to get the invitation.

57.4 Using adjective clauses appropriately

Revise the following sentences so that each includes an appropriate adjective clause that is positioned correctly. Make sure the sentence does not include unnecessary words or omit necessary relative pronouns. If a sentence does not contain an error, write C. (See *The Everyday Writer*, section 57e.) Example:

     who
The student works the hardest gains the most.
      ^

1. The class has twenty students in it that I am taking.

2. Some students want to practice speaking more asked us all to help prepare a dinner.

3. The class dinner we cooked together represented food from a dozen countries.

4. A reporter attended the dinner and wrote an article which he praised the chefs in it.

5. The chef works at my club helped by lending us pots and pans.

6. My mother makes many delicious dishes that they come from our homeland.

7. She taught me how to make that I have always loved the fritters called *kofte*.

8. We all come from different places, so those of us were cooking together had to speak English to communicate.

9. The room in that we made our dinner smelled delicious.

10. Spoken English, which I had always found very difficult, is easier for me now.

57.5 Writing conditional sentences

Revise each of the following sentences so that both the *if* clause and the main, or independent, clause contain appropriate verb forms. If a sentence does not contain an error, write C. (See *The Everyday Writer*, section 57f.) Example:

> **If you want to work as a computer programmer, you ~~would~~**
> are
> **probably ~~be~~ having a hard time finding a high-paying U.S. job**
> ^
> **these days.**

1. Until recently, many people thought that U.S. computer jobs will go unfilled unless college-educated foreign workers will be allowed to work in this country.

2. If the dot-com boom had continued, that prediction might come true.

3. Instead, many highly skilled U.S. technology workers will have few options if they became unemployed tomorrow.

4. If any computer job is announced these days, hundreds of qualified people applied for it.

5. Today, if a company uses many programmers or other computer experts, it may hire workers in India to fill the positions.

6. If Indian workers would require as much money as Americans do to live, U.S. companies would not be as eager to outsource computer work to the other side of the world.

7. If business owners cared more about keeping good jobs at home, they hired skilled workers here instead of skilled workers in another country.

8. Will fewer Americans be unemployed right now if the dot-com boom had never happened?

9. Some young people in this country would not have gotten useless technology degrees if they knew how the economy would decline.

10. If American students would want to prepare for a secure future, they should consider a specialty like nursing, in which jobs are available and the work cannot be sent abroad.

58.1 Identifying count and noncount nouns

Identify each of the common nouns in the following short paragraph as either a count or a noncount noun. (See *The Everyday Writer,* section 58a.) The first one has been done for you.

>   *count*
> In his <u>book</u> *Hiroshima*, John Hersey tells the story of six people who
> survived the destruction of Hiroshima on August 6, 1945. The bomb deto-
> nated at 8:15 in the morning. When the explosion occurred, Mrs. Hatsuyo
> Nakamura was looking out her window and watching a neighbor at work
> on his house. The force of the explosion lifted her into the air and carried her
> into the next room, where she was buried by roofing tiles and other debris.
> When she crawled out, she heard her daughter, Myeko, calling out; she was
> buried up to her waist and could not move.

58.2 Using determiners appropriately; using articles conventionally

Each of the following sentences contains an error with a noun phrase. Revise each sentence. (See *The Everyday Writer,* sections 58c and d.) Example:

>   *a*
> **Many people use small sponge to clean their kitchen counters.**
>   ^

1. Bacteria are invisible organisms that can sometimes make the people sick.

2. Dangerous germs such as salmonella are commonly found in a some foods.

3. When a cook prepares chicken on cutting board, salmonella germs may be left on the board.

4. Much people regularly clean their kitchen counters and cutting boards to remove bacteria.

5. Unfortunately, a warm, wet kitchen sponge is a ideal home for bacteria.

6. Every time someone wipes a counter with dirty sponge, more germ are spread around the kitchen.

7. Microwaving a dirty sponge for one minute will kill a most bacteria that live in it.

8. According to research studies, the young single men's kitchens tend to have a fewer germs than many other kitchen.

9. These surprising fact tells researchers that young single men do not often wipe their kitchen counters.

10. To eliminate dangerous many bacteria from the kitchen, a cooks should wash their hands frequently.

58.3 Using articles appropriately

Insert articles as necessary in the following passage. If no article is needed, leave the space blank. (See *The Everyday Writer*, section 58d.) Example:

One of _____the_____ things that makes _____ English unique is

_____the_____ number of _____ English words.

_____ English language has _____ very large vocabu-

lary. About _____ 200,000 words are in _____ everyday use,

and if _____ less common words are included, _____ total

reaches more than _____ million. This makes _____ English

_____ rich language, but also _____ difficult one to learn well.

In addition, _____ rules of English grammar are sometimes confusing.

They were modeled on _____ Latin rules, even though _____

two languages are very different. Finally, _____ fact that _____

English has _____ large number of _____ words imported

from _____ other languages makes _____ English spelling very

hard to master. _____ English is now _____ most widely used

language around _____ world, so _____ educated people are

expected to know it.

58.4 Positioning modifiers

Possible modifiers for each of the following nouns are listed alpha-
betically in parentheses after the noun. Indicate the order in which the
adjectives should precede the noun. (See *The Everyday Writer,* section 58e.)
Example:

 Popular New Orleans jazz **album (jazz/New Orleans/popular)**

1. _____ mansion (old/creaky)

2. _____ mining town (uninhabited/dusty/dry)

3. _____ movie (moving/poignant/epic)

4. _____ beach (local/crowded)

5. _____ cloud (threatening/storm)

6. _____ team (coed/volleyball)

7. _____ cloth (batik/orange/unusual)

8. _____ program (educational/worthwhile)

9. _____ pumpkin (orange/fat)

10. _____ rental (movie/X-rated)

59.1 Using the present, the present perfect, and the past forms of verbs

Rewrite the following passage by adding appropriate forms of *have* and main-verb endings or forms for the verbs in parentheses. (See *The Everyday Writer,* Chapter 59.) Example:

I _____*like*_____ (like) to try new foods, so I ____*have eaten*____

(eat) in many different kinds of restaurants in my life.

Several times, I _____ (hear) people musing about

the bravery of the first person who ever _____ (eat) a

lobster. It _____ (be) an interesting question: what do you

_____ (think) _____ (make) anyone do such a

thing? But personally, I _____ (wonder) all my life about how

ancient people _____ (discover) the art of baking bread. After

all, preparing a lobster _____ (be) pretty simple in comparison

to baking. Bread _____ (feed) vast numbers of people for

centuries, so it certainly _____ (be) a more important food

source than lobster, too. Those of us who _____ (love) either

lobster or bread (or both) _____ (be) grateful to those who

_____ (give) us such a wonderful culinary legacy.

59.2 Using specified forms of verbs

Using the subjects and verbs provided, write the specified sentences. (See *The Everyday Writer,* Chapter 59.) Example:

subject: *Bernie* **verb:** *touch*
sentence using a present form: Bernie touches the soft fur.
sentence using the auxiliary verb *had***:** Bernie had touched a squid before.

1. subject: *Professor Jones* verb: *teach*

   sentence using a past form:

   sentence using an auxiliary verb + the past participle form:

2. subject: *dogs* verb: *bark*

   sentence using a past form:

   sentence using the auxiliary *were* + the present participle form:

3. subject: *The student* verb: *dream*

   sentence using a present form:

   sentence using an auxiliary verb + the past participle form:

4. subject: *I* verb: *bring*

   sentence using a past form:

   sentence using the auxiliary *be* + the present participle form:

5. subject: *baby* verb: *sleep*

   sentence using a present form:

   sentence using an auxiliary verb + past participle form:

6. subject: *teenagers* verb: *consume*

   sentence using a past form:

   sentence using the auxiliary verb *were* + the present participle form:

7. subject: *judge* verb: *expect*

   sentence using a present form:

   sentence using an auxiliary verb + the present participle form:

8. subject: *pasta* verb: *steam*

   sentence using a past form:

   sentence using an auxiliary verb + the present participle form:

9. subject: *pilots* verb: *fly*

   sentence using a past form:

   sentence using an auxiliary verb + the present participle form:

10. subject: *hamburger* verb: *taste*

    sentence using a present form:

    sentence using an auxiliary verb + the past participle form:

59.3 Identifying tenses and forms of verbs

From the following list, identify the form of each verb or verb phrase in each of the numbered sentences. (See *The Everyday Writer,* Chapter 59.)

simple present	past perfect
simple past	present progressive
present perfect	past progressive

Example:

> **Judge Cohen considered the two arguments.** Simple past

1. Paul is painting the bedroom, and it looks great so far.

2. She was walking to work when the first plane struck the Twin Towers.

3. By the late 1980s, R.E.M. had become a very popular band.

4. She has admired you for years.

5. Just as we took our seats, the movie began.

6. I have attempted that math problem several times now.

7. Paul required special medical attention for years.

8. My mother has driven the same Mazda for ten years.

9. Horror movies rarely make much of an impression on me, but this one has made me afraid to go out into the parking lot.

10. She had forgotten the assignment.

59.4 Using verbs appropriately

Each of the following sentences contains an error with verbs. Revise each sentence. (See *The Everyday Writer*, Chapter 59.) Example:

could not
Linguists ~~cannot~~ interpret hieroglyphics before they discovered the
                  ^
Rosetta Stone.

1. A French engineer was finding a stone half-buried in the mud by the Nile River in Egypt in 1799.

2. The Rosetta Stone is cover with inscriptions in three ancient languages.

3. The inscription at the top of the stone written in Egyptian hieroglyphics, or pictographs, while the lower part gives the same information in an ancient Egyptian language called Demotic and in ancient Greek.

4. At that time, scholars were puzzled by hieroglyphics for centuries.

5. Very soon after its discovery, the French have made copies of the stone.

6. A scholar named Jean François Champollion could understood both ancient Greek and modern Egyptian, known as Coptic.

7. Champollion knew that he can figure out the Demotic script based on his knowledge of Coptic.

8. From the Coptic inscription, he has learned to read the hieroglyphics.

9. The story of the Rosetta Stone is probably more fascinated than the contents of its inscription.

10. The hieroglyphics, Demotic, and Greek texts all are containing a decree from an ancient king.

60.1 Using prepositions idiomatically

Insert one or more appropriate prepositions in each of the following sentences. (See *The Everyday Writer*, section 60a.) Example:

We will have the answer ____by____ four o'clock this afternoon.

1. Shall we eat _____ the restaurant, or would you prefer to take food

   _____ ?

2. I hate driving _____ the city _____ rush hour.

3. Have you ever fallen _____ love at first sight?

4. To get to my house, drive _____ Valley Road and make a right

   _____ Cherry Street.

5. Adults who read to children can provide good examples _____

   them.

6. Students should get to school precisely _____ time.

7. Having someone to help them _____ home gives struggling

   students more confidence.

8. Schools themselves may be struggling _____ financial cutbacks

   and poor facilities.

9. Classrooms need books _____ their shelves.

10. A high-quality public education should be given _____ every child.

60.2 Recognizing and using two-word verbs

Identify each italicized expression as either a two-word verb or a verb + preposition. (See *The Everyday Writer*, section 60b.) Example:

Look up John Brown the next time you're in town.   two-word verb

1. George was still *looking for* his keys when we left.

2. I always *turn down* the thermostat when I go to bed or leave the house.

3. We drank a pitcher of lemonade in an attempt to *cool* ourselves *off* on a sweltering July afternoon.

4. Marion *gave back* the ring she had gotten as an engagement gift.

5. Jimmy *takes after* his father, poor thing.

6. The car *turned into* the driveway.

7. The frog *turned into* a prince.

8. The camp counselor *handed* the candy *out* as if it were gold.

9. *Put* the garbage *out* on the sidewalk, please.

10. Don't *put* yourself *out* on my behalf.

Answers to the Even-Numbered Exercises

WRITING FOR COLLEGE AND BEYOND

EXERCISE 1.1 The top twenty: A quick guide to troubleshooting your writing

Some sentences have errors that most people would solve the same way; some sentences contain errors that have various solutions. Students may wish to make changes in addition to the corrections noted.

2. [wrong word] Popular spring break **destinations** over the years have included Mexican resorts, Florida beaches, and Caribbean islands.

4. [sentence fragment] A new trend, known as alternative spring breaks, allows college students to contribute their time to humanitarian causes **or** environmental organizations.

6. [poorly integrated quotation] There are a host of options available to students who want to volunteer over their spring break. **According to one online student newspaper,** "Programs range from working with kids in U.S. cities to building sustainable water systems in Nicaragua" (Delgado).

8. [vague pronoun reference] Students can find the best match for their interests and desired location with the help of large nonprofit organizations such as United Way. **These organizations** also frequently subsidize the costs of the trips to make them more affordable.

10. [fused sentence] Some students work within their own communities; others may travel thousands of miles to volunteer over spring break.

12. [faulty sentence structure] In Michigan, students renovated a community recreation center and added a reading corner to encourage children to read after school each day.

14. [missing commas with a nonrestrictive element] On the Gulf Coast, where the 2010 oil spill devastated shorelines, students have helped clean up beaches and safeguard sea turtle nests.

16. [missing comma in a compound sentence] All students have their own reasons for embarking on an alternative spring break, but many find that they come away with benefits they had not anticipated.

18. [mechanical error with a quotation] Moreover, as noted in a United Way blog entry, "What many students don't realize until they arrive is the impact it will have on their own lives" ("We Did Not Give Up").

20. [missing comma after introductory element] Another student Delgado interviewed found that through helping others he was actually helping himself. After volunteering with poor families in south Mississippi, he realized how fortunate he was and gained a better sense of his priorities in life ("Because Partying Is Too Mainstream").

CRITICAL THINKING AND ARGUMENT

EXERCISE 13.2 Recognizing fallacies

SUGGESTED ANSWERS

2. *In-crowd appeal:* This argument suggests to readers that they can be part of the financially successful crowd if they visit a particular Web site.

4. *Bandwagon appeal:* This passage uses "peer pressure" to convince the reader to watch the new television show.

6. *Flattery:* This argument tries to persuade the reader that because he or she is sensible about savings, he or she should invest in gold.

8. *Oversimplification:* It is a vast oversimplification to claim that legalizing marijuana would completely eradicate drug problems in this country.

10. *Either-or fallacy:* The writer suggests that the only possible route into an Ivy League college is by graduating from an elite private high school, as if no other high school graduates attend Ivy League schools.

EXERCISE 14.1 Recognizing arguable statements

2.	factual	8.	arguable
4.	factual	10.	arguable
6.	factual		

EXERCISE 14.2 Demonstrating fairness

SUGGESTED ANSWERS

2. The writers demonstrate fairness by explaining that the volunteer depicted in the advertisement gives just a few hours of her day to support youth literacy, which makes the volunteer time commitment reasonable for most people. The writers also point out that Ruth Rusie's efforts are improving the education, income, and health of her community.

LANGUAGE

EXERCISE 21.1 Identifying stereotypes

2. Assumes that *all* women enjoy a particular kind of literature (and that no men do).

4. Implies that a chiropractor is not a legitimate medical practitioner.

6. Suggests that offensive and inappropriate behavior is somehow excusable because of gender predisposition to act a certain way.

8. Assumes that third-graders could be attentive, focused, and calm only with the help of pharmaceuticals.

EXERCISE 21.3 Rewriting to eliminate offensive references

SUGGESTED ANSWERS

2. All of the children in the kindergarten class will ask someone at home to help make cookies for the bake sale.

4. Acting as a spokesperson, Cynthia McDowell vowed that all elementary schoolteachers in the district would take their turns on the picket line until the school board agreed to resume negotiations.

6. Violinist Josh Mickle, last night's featured soloist, brought the crowd to its feet. (Or accept any version that omits mention of age and religion—both irrelevant here.)

8. The interdenominational service was attended by people of Jewish, Christian, Buddhist, and Islamic faiths.

10. Attorney Margaret Samuelson won her sixteenth case in a row last week.

EXERCISE 23.1 Using appropriate formality

SUGGESTED ANSWERS

2. I agree with many of his environmental policies, but that proposal is absolutely absurd.

4. We decided not to buy a bigger car that got terrible gas mileage and instead to keep our old Honda.

6. After she had raced to the post office at ten minutes to five, she realized that she had completely forgotten the fact that it was a federal holiday.

8. Moby Dick's enormous size was matched only by Ahab's obsessive desire to destroy him.

10. The class misbehaved so dreadfully in their regular teacher's absence that the substitute lost his temper.

EXERCISE 23.2 Determining levels of language

SUGGESTED ANSWERS

2. formal; *audience:* a prospective employer you want to impress

4. formal; *audience:* an informed audience whom you hope to convince

EXERCISE 23.3 Checking for correct denotation

2. abdicate; Correct word: *advocate*

4. exuded; Correct word: *excluded*

6. Correct

8. comprise; Correct word: *compromise*

10. avoidable; Correct word: *available*

EXERCISE 23.4 Revising sentences to change connotations

2. waltz away/little people who keep the company running/peanuts
   Rewrite: CEOs are highly compensated with salary, stock options, and pension funds while employees get comparatively little.

4. Tree-huggers/ranted
   Rewrite: Environmentalists protested the Explorer's gas mileage outside the Ford dealership.

6. Naive/stumble/blithely yank
   Rewrite: Often voters not familiar with using a voting machine will simply pull the handle without making informed choices.

8. mob/yelling/jabbing
   Rewrite: A large group of chanting, sign-waving protesters appeared.

EXERCISE 23.5 Considering connotation

SUGGESTED ANSWERS

2. *girl:* young lady, miss

4. *abide:* tolerate; *turns:* changes; *vital:* alive; *hold still:* contain their energy

EXERCISE 23.6 Using specific and concrete words

SUGGESTED ANSWERS

2. Despite her hunger after having fasted for twenty-four hours, she stared at the menu as if in a trance, unable to decide which of the fifteen mouthwatering entrées would best satisfy her appetite.

4. The crumbling stone castle rising up on the mossy plateau adjacent to Loch Sween is believed to have been built by the Celts in the middle of the ninth century.

6. A week's worth of laundry lay scattered on the floor, the unmade beds showed off our wrinkled sheets, and dishes from late-night snacking covered our desks.

8. Oozing with a rich, warm center and dusted with powdered sugar, the chocolate lava cake was irresistible.

10. Every day after school, Tyler gets suited up, grabs his skateboard, and heads to the skate park where he practices his spins, flips, and jaywalks in the cement half-pipes.

EXERCISE 23.7 Thinking about similes and metaphors

SUGGESTED ANSWERS

2. *like a football game and he's quarterbacking the underdog team* (simile): compares marriage to a team sport with rough play, strategy, and winners and losers.

4. *like microscopic pieces of a jigsaw puzzle* (simile): helps the reader visualize the way sensory information is processed by the brain.

6. *like a sheet of metal* (simile): expresses the cold, hard grayness of the sky, implying severity and a sense of foreboding.

8. *like malaria; Like a virus that lingers in the body and returns to haunt you* (simile): illuminates the character's negative feeling about a memory by comparing it to a disease that will not go away.

10. *like a segment of tangerine* (simile): clarifies the sun's unusual shape by comparing it to a familiar food item.

EXERCISE 23.8 Recognizing correct spellings

2. foods	8. says; passed
4. There; including	10. fruit
6. too; tried	

EXERCISE 23.11 Spelling plurals

2. curricula	8. spies
4. wolves	10. boxes
6. men-of-war	12. mothers-in-law

EXERCISE 24.1 Selecting the appropriate word

2. farther	12. may
4. fewer; than	14. continuous
6. discreet	16. with
8. lend	18. flaunts
10. bad	20. whether or not

EXERCISE 24.2 Editing inappropiate words

2. Ryan went to the writing center to get some *advice* on improving his research paper.

4. On a sunny day Mt. Rainier gives the *illusion* of floating in air just south of Seattle.

6. Quinn felt *bad* about losing the game, but she knew she had tried her best.

8. Shows that air on television before 10:00 PM must be *censored* if they contain profane language.

10. While waiting at the gate for my plane, I was *conscious* of a suitcase that had been left unattended for more than ten minutes.

12. Correct

14. There are definitely *fewer* cookies on the plate now than there were this morning.

16. Ideally, a puppy shouldn't be separated from *its* mother until it is eight weeks old.

18. The *moral* of the story is that crime does not pay.

20. The reason I canceled my Facebook account was *that* it interfered with my studying.

SENTENCE STYLE

EXERCISE 25.2 Writing sentences with subordination

SUGGESTED ANSWERS

2. Although an umbrella can keep you cool at the beach, it can't completely protect you from the sun because the rays reflect from the sand onto your skin, so you still need to wear sunscreen.

4. My sister thinks reality television shows are completely unscripted, but I think many of the people are actually acting so viewers will be drawn in by the drama.

EXERCISE 25.4 Emphasizing main ideas

SUGGESTED ANSWERS

2. Ever since the iPhone became popular, apps have been created that allow us to play games, record voice memos, and instantly recognize constellations in the night sky.

4. The word *marathon*, as many people have heard, comes from the ancient Greek legend that a runner delivered a victory message from the Battle of Marathon to Athens, which was twenty-six miles away.

6. Born in Austria in 1756 and having written enduringly popular operas, concertos, and symphonies, Mozart is perhaps the greatest composer of all time.

8. Even though it is tall and appears to have leaves and a trunk, the palm tree is not a tree.

10. This all-in-one plant food I bought kept the bugs away, prevented fungus from forming, and led to the largest tomato crop I have ever seen.

EXERCISE 26.1   Matching subjects and predicates

SUGGESTED ANSWERS

2. In her books, many of which deal with the aftermath of slavery, are strong women characters.

   Her books, many of which deal with the aftermath of slavery, often feature strong women characters.

4. Although Morrison's depictions of African American families and neighborhoods are realistic, they also include supernatural elements.

   Morrison's depictions of African American families and neighborhoods are realistic, but they also include supernatural elements.

6. *Song of Solomon* was hailed as a masterpiece, winning the National Book Critics Circle Award in 1978.

   Song of Solomon, hailed as a masterpiece, won the National Book Critics Circle Award in 1978.

8. The title character in *Beloved* is the ghost of a murdered infant inhabiting the body of a young woman.

   Beloved features the ghost of a murdered infant inhabiting the body of a young woman.

10. In 1993, Toni Morrison became the first African American woman to be awarded the Nobel Prize in literature.

   Toni Morrison, who was awarded the Nobel Prize in literature in 1993, was the first African American woman to win that prize.

EXERCISE 26.2   Making comparisons complete, consistent, and clear

SUGGESTED ANSWERS

2. Records show that the average sea temperature in the past decade is higher than it has ever been.

4. 3-D movies these days are a bit blurry, but they are still better than they were in the 1950s.

6. Travel on a commercial airplane is statistically safer than travel in a car.

8. Alligators typically have more teeth than crocodiles do.

10. Is the U.S. national debt higher than the debt of other countries?

EXERCISE 27.1 Creating parallel words or phrases

SUGGESTED ANSWERS

2. This summer, I want to learn to knit, to visit my grandparents, and to earn money for college.

4. In preparation for his wedding day, the groom rented a tux, chose his best man, and hired a band.

6. When he got his promotion, he told the neighbors, called his family, and took out an ad in the newspaper.

8. The college athlete realized she would need to both practice longer and study harder.

10. Just as the demand for qualified teachers has increased, so has the supply dwindled.

EXERCISE 27.2 Revising sentences for parallelism

SUGGESTED ANSWERS

2. Many people in this country remember dancing to the mambo music of the 1950s and listening to that era's Latin bands.

4. Growing up near Havana and studying classical piano, Pérez Prado loved Cuban music.

6. Playing piano in Havana nightclubs, arranging music for a Latin big band, and joining jam sessions with the band's guitarists gave him the idea for a new kind of music.

8. Prado conducted his orchestra by waving his hands, moving his head and shoulders, and kicking his feet high in the air.

10. Pérez Prado, an innovator and a great musician, died in 1989.

EXERCISE 28.1 Revising for verb tense and mood

SUGGESTED ANSWERS

2. I waited for almost forty-five minutes on hold, but after a while I gave up hope.

4. In business courses, they teach you that your customer list is your greatest asset and that the customer is always right!

6. Correct

8. If their product is defective, why should I waste my time trying to repair it?

10. Finally, I hung up the phone, drove to the computer store, and got my money back.

EXERCISE 28.2 Eliminating shifts in voice and point of view

SUGGESTED ANSWERS

2. I had planned to walk home after the movie, but I knew I shouldn't be on campus alone after dark.

4. Instructors at the studio cooperative offer a wide variety of dance lessons as well as art and voice training.

6. The twenty-four-hour cable news channel is not all that new; it has been around for over thirty years.

8. Some members of the group took ziplining lessons while others went on a rapids ride.

10. The slow food movement emerged in France several decades ago; it set out to oppose the spread of fast-food chains in Europe.

EXERCISE 28.3 Eliminating shifts between direct and indirect discourse

SUGGESTED ANSWERS

2. She said that during a semester abroad, *she really missed all her friends.*

4. Loren Eiseley feels an urge to join the birds in their soundless flight, but in the end he knows that he cannot *and that he is only a man.*

EXERCISE 28.4 Eliminating shifts in tone and word choice

SUGGESTED ANSWERS

2. The novel concludes without tying up all of the loose ends, which would be tolerable if the narrator hadn't trailed too far off the main premise of the book.

4. Once I get sucked into a video game, I find it hard to stop.

EXERCISE 29.1 Eliminating unnecessary words and phrases

SUGGESTED ANSWERS

2. Shortly after Houdini's birth, his family moved to Appleton, where his father served as the only rabbi.

4. His many escapes included getting out of a giant sealed envelope without tearing it and walking out of jail cells that were said to be escapeproof.

6. Clearly, Houdini did not want anyone to know his secrets.

8. Houdini's tremendous control over almost every muscle allowed him to contort his body into seemingly impossible positions.

10. On his deathbed, Houdini promised his wife that he would try to make contact with her from beyond the grave, but so far, he has never been able to get in touch.

SENTENCE GRAMMAR

EXERCISE 31.1 Identifying subjects and predicates

The subject is set in *italics;* the predicate is set in **boldface.**

2. *It* **was an immense crowd, two thousand at the least and growing every minute.**

4. **In a job like that,** *you* **see the dirty work of Empire at close quarters.**

6. *The hangman, a gray-haired convict in the white uniform of the prison,* **was waiting beside his machine.**

8. **Would** *I* **please come and do something about it?**

10. *We* **set out for the gallows.**

EXERCISE 31.2 Identifying verbs and verb phrases

2. Holi <u>is known</u> as the festival of colors, not only because spring <u>brings</u> flowers, but also because Holi celebrations always <u>include</u> brightly colored dyes.

4. During Holi, people <u>toss</u> fistfuls of powdered dyes or dye-filled water balloons at each other and <u>sing</u> traditional Holi songs.

6. Any person who <u>is walking</u> outside during a Holi celebration <u>will</u> soon <u>be wearing</u> colored powders or colored water.

8. Most people <u>wear</u> white clothing for Holi.

10. Doesn't Holi <u>sound</u> like fun?

EXERCISE 31.3 Identifying nouns and articles

Nouns are set in *italics;* articles are set in **boldface.**

2. **the;** *music*

4. *papers; semester; exams*

6. **the;** *United States;* **the;** *end;* **the;** *century; people;* **a;** *phone;* **a;** *computer;* **a;** *camera*

8. *Harry Potter's world; owls;* **the;** *mail; goblins;* **the;** *bank*

10. **A;** *television; power*

EXERCISE 31.4 Identifying pronouns and antecedents

Pronouns are set in *italics;* antecedents are set in **boldface.**

2. **dogs;** *that; their*

4. *they; their;* **volunteers; puppy;** *its*

6. *you*; **puppy**; *its*; **coat**; *that*; *it*

8. *Some*; **pups**; *these*

10. *you*; *your*

EXERCISE 31.5 Identifying adjectives and adverbs

Adjectives are set in *italics*; adverbs are set in **boldface.**

2. **nearly**; *twenty*; *the*; **wrongfully**; *accused*

4. **Moreover**; *some*; *talk-show*; **intentionally**; *the*; *misleading*

6. *Color*; *laser*; **not**; **very**; *expensive*; *the*; *ink*; *your*

8. *The*; *rusty*; *old*; *swing*

10. **quite**; *handy*; *landscaping*

EXERCISE 31.6 Adding adjectives and adverbs

SUGGESTED ANSWERS

2. Surely, most of us enjoy classic movies.

4. A multinational corporation can fire undependable workers.

6. The unpopulated boardwalk crosses the bleak, wintry beach.

8. The mainstream media are determinedly ignoring his candidacy.

10. Which way did you say the hunted pair went yesterday?

EXERCISE 31.7 Identifying prepositions

2. upon; into; as

4. Due to; through; with

6. In spite of; from; below

8. with; above; of; up; beyond

10. From; upon; in; of

EXERCISE 31.8 Identifying conjunctions

2. Not only. . . but also [two parts of a correlative conjunction]; and

4. When; and

6. but; and

8. either . . . or [two parts of a correlative conjunction]

10. After; and; whether . . . or [two parts of a correlative conjunction]

EXERCISE 31.9 Identifying conjunctions and interjections

2. Although (SUBORD)

4. after (SUBORD); Ouch (interjection)

6. Until (SUBORD)

8. Aha (interjection); but (COORD)

10. so (COORD)

EXERCISE 31.10 Identifying the parts of speech

2. *Although*—conjunction (subordinating); *we*—pronoun (personal); *of*—preposition; *not*—adverb

4. *large*—adjective; *exceptionally*—adverb; *England*—noun (proper); *used*—verb

6. *The*—article (adjective); *continues*—verb

8. *It*—pronoun (personal); *before*—preposition

10. *Incidentally*—conjunctive adverb; *did contract*—verb; *this*—pronoun (demonstrative); *the lead*—adjective

EXERCISE 31.11 Identifying subjects

Complete subjects are set in *italics;* simple subjects are set in **boldface.**

2. *Ancient Chinese, Greeks, and Romans, as well as South and Central Americans,* **all** played versions of "football."

4. In 1863, *eleven London soccer* **clubs** sent their representatives to the Freemason's Tavern for a meeting.

6. In the minority were *the* **proponents** *of rugby,* who were against rules that forbade ball-carrying.

8. *The historical* **meeting** led to the eventual split between rugby and football, and to the founding of the Football Association.

10. **It** is the most widely watched sporting event in the world.

EXERCISE 31.12 Identifying predicates

Predicates are set in *italics.*

2. *retested* [TV] *the subjects* [DO]

4. *published* [TV] *their findings about the effects of the music* [DO] *in a scholarly journal*

6. *fed* [TV] *people* [IO] *stories about the amazing intelligence-boosting properties of classical music* [DO]

8. *was* [LV] *born* [SC]

10. *rejected* [TV] *the commercialization of their findings* [DO]

EXERCISE 31.13 Identifying prepositional phrases

2. from Italy; in an overcrowded boat; among his countrymen and women

4. Without any formal education; against all odds; in business

EXERCISE 31.14 Using prepositional phrases

SUGGESTED ANSWERS

2. Polytetrafluoroethylene (PTFE) is the chemical name for Teflon.

4. The substance allows food to cook in a pan without sticking.

6. Early nonstick cookware coating tended to peel off the surface of the pan at the slightest touch of a metal utensil.

8. The primer holds the PTFE coat in place with a physical bond, not a chemical one.

10. As an adjective, the word *Teflon* describes a person who seems to get out of sticky situations easily.

EXERCISE 31.15 Identifying verbal phrases

2. infinitive—*to write articles about their lives and publish them online*

4. participial—*searching very hard*; participial—*inspired by military service*; participial—*focused on careers*; participial—*dedicated to cooking*

6. participial—*targeted to a specific audience of readers who are known and trusted*

8. gerund—*spending too much time online*

10. infinitive—*to balance our online worlds with our real worlds*; infinitive—*to have a healthy and realistic outlook on life*

EXERCISE 31.16 Identifying prepositional, verbal, absolute, and appositive phrases

2. verbal—*outlined against the sky*; prep—*against the sky*; verbal—*to move*

4. absolute—*her fingers clutching the fence*; verbal—*clutching the fence*

6. verbal—*Floating on my back*; prep—*on my back*

8. app—*the leader of the group*; prep—*of the group*; verbal—*to relinquish any authority*

10. verbal—*Shocked into silence*; prep—*into silence*; verbal—*fixed on the odd creature*; prep—*on the odd creature*

EXERCISE 31.17 Adding prepositional, verbal, absolute, and appositive phrases

Suggested Answers

2. Known primarily for her screen roles and good looks, the actress ran for political office.

4. Squealing all the way down the hill, Brent's car won the soap box derby.

6. Melissa, valedictorian and captain of the field hockey team, was not accepted into Yale.

8. We attended the convention to learn more about careers in the health care field.

10. Joining a fraternity, I decided, would interfere with my schoolwork.

EXERCISE 31.18 Using verbal, absolute, and appositive phrases to combine sentences

Suggested Answers

2. If you plan to fly into Dublin, you can backpack your way around the country from there.

4. The Ballsbridge area, home to foreign embassies and many other sites, is another fine place to visit.

6. The Irish National Gallery, worth checking out for art lovers, is located at Merrion Square West.

8. Stand on the Martello Tower in Sandycove, the Irish Sea before you.

10. Saying good-bye to Dublin will be difficult, but there is much more of the country to explore.

EXERCISE 31.19 Identifying dependent clauses

Dependent clauses are set in *italics.*

2. *when spring arrives in the South;* sub conj—when

4. *Although the Appalachian mountain range has relatively low peaks;* sub conj—Although

6. *Because the Appalachian Trail lies mainly in wilderness;* sub conj—Because

8. *that have become accustomed to humans;* rel pron—that

10. *how to react to an aggressive bear to minimize the danger;* rel pron—how

EXERCISE 31.20 Adding dependent clauses

Suggested Answers

2. Everyone in a family that spends the day in separate places may have high expectations for time together.

4. Whining, which all children do from time to time, is difficult to listen to and easy to stop with a new toy or an extra video viewing.

6. Misbehaving children who expect to get their own way wear out their welcome quickly.

8. Parents who want to set a good example must learn to stick to their own rules.

10. Even if children protest against discipline, which everyone resists from time to time, they want to know how to behave.

EXERCISE 31.21 Distinguishing between phrases and clauses

Dependent clauses are set in *italics;* phrases are set in **boldface.**

2. **as beyond recall, beyond recall**—prep phrases

4. **of encountering a Perelman piece**—prep phrase; **encountering a Perelman piece**—verbal phrase; **in a magazine**—prep phrase

6. **at a glance**—prep phrase; *that Professor Strunk omitted needless words*

8. *When I start a book; what my characters are going to do;* **to do**—verbal; **for their eccentric behavior**—prep phrase

10. *When I wrote "Death of a Pig";* **of a Pig**—prep phrase; **of what actually happened**—prep phrase; **on my place**—prep phrase; **to my pig**—prep phrase; *who died;* **to me**—prep phrase; *who tended him;* **in his last hours**—prep phrase

Imitation sentences will vary.

EXERCISE 31.22 Classifying sentences grammatically and functionally

2. complex, declarative
8. compound, declarative
4. compound-complex, declarative
10. simple, exclamatory
6. complex, declarative

EXERCISE 32.1 Using irregular verb forms

2. was; said; was
8. kept; was
4. broke; lay
10. grown; spread
6. met; fell

EXERCISE 32.2 Editing verb forms

2. have wen—went
8. swum—swam
4. Correct
10. lend—lent
6. knew—known

EXERCISE 32.3   Distinguishing between *lie* and *lay*, *sit* and *set*, *rise* and *raise*

2.   laid
4.   Sit
6.   lie

8.   raise
10. rose

EXERCISE 32.4   Deciding on verb tenses

2.   begin; dates
4.   have opened
6.   was looking; suggested

8.   are searching; requires
10. will check; is teaching

EXERCISE 32.5   Sequencing tenses

2.   Until I *started* knitting again last month, I *had forgotten* how.
4.   After Darius said that he wanted to postpone college, I *tried* to talk him out of it.
6.   I *had imagined* the job *would be finished* by that point.
8.   When he *was* twenty-one, he *wanted* to *become* a millionaire by the age of thirty.
10.   *Having worked* at the law firm for five years, she *was* ready for a change.

EXERCISE 32.6   Converting the voice of a sentence

Answers may vary slightly.

2.   The protesting students *were mistreated* by campus security.
4.   My mother *cooked* my favorite dinner on my birthday.
6.   Storms all across the country *are being* caused by an unusual weather pattern.
8.   The flight attendants *were ordered* to take their seats by the captain.
10.   My blood pressure *was taken* by the nurse.

EXERCISE 32.7   Using subjunctive mood

2.   was—were
4.   was—were
6.   was—were
8.   tells—tell
10.   should not wear—not wear

EXERCISE 33.1 Selecting verbs that agree with their subjects

2. are

4. have

6. is

8. was

10. has

EXERCISE 33.2 Making subjects and verbs agree

2. are—is

4. use—uses

6. sets—set

8. Correct

10. allows—allow

12. Correct

14. belongs—belong

EXERCISE 34.1 Using subjective case pronouns

2. it

4. we

6. she

8. we

10. he

EXERCISE 34.2 Using objective case pronouns

2. Correct

4. When we asked, the seller promised <u>us</u> that the software would work on a Macintosh computer.

6. The teacher praised <u>them</u> for asking thoughtful questions.

8. Correct

10. I couldn't tell who was more to blame for the accident, <u>you</u> or Susan.

EXERCISE 34.3 Using possessive case pronouns

2. mine

4. Her

6. their

8. her

10. yours

EXERCISE 34.4 Using *who, whoever, whom,* or *whomever*

2. whoever

4. whoever

6. Whom

8. who

10. whoever

EXERCISE 34.5   Using pronouns in compound structures, appositives, elliptical clauses; choosing between *we* and *us* before a noun

2.	he	10.	he
4.	him	12.	us
6.	her	14.	I
8.	them		

EXERCISE 34.6   Maintaining pronoun-antecedent agreement

SUGGESTED ANSWERS

2. A family that is prone to allergies may have a higher than usual percentage of allergic diseases, but its specific allergies are not necessarily the same for all family members.

4. Because of the severity and frequency of nut allergies in small children, day-care centers typically have rules specifying that they cannot allow any nut products.

6. Even at the elementary school level, a class that shares a common snack may ask parents to avoid sending in nut products for its students.

8. Correct

10. One alternative idea to the total nut ban is the creation of "nut-free zones," where children with allergies can safely eat their food without any exposure to nuts.

EXERCISE 34.7   Clarifying pronoun reference

SUGGESTED ANSWERS

2. Not long after the company set up the subsidiary, the subsidiary went bankrupt.

   Not long after the company set up the subsidiary, the company went bankrupt.

4. When Deyon was reunited with his father, the boy wept.

   When Deyon was reunited with his father, his father wept.

6. The weather forecast said to expect snow in the overnight hours.

8. Lear divides his kingdom between the two older daughters, Goneril and Regan, whose extravagant professions of love are more flattering than the simple affection of the youngest daughter, Cordelia. The consequences of this error in judgment soon become apparent, as the older daughters prove neither grateful nor kind to him.

10. The visit to the pyramids was canceled because of the recent terrorist attacks on tourists there, so Kay, who had waited years to see the monuments, was disappointed.

EXERCISE 35.1 Using adjectives and adverbs appropriately

2. defiant—defiantly; modifies *crosses*

4. sadly—sad; modifies *you*

6. relievedly—relieved; modifies *you*

8. oddly—odd; modifies *"words"*

10. Lucky—Luckily; modifies *available*

EXERCISE 35.2 Using comparative and superlative modifiers appropriately

SUGGESTED ANSWERS

2. the famousest—the most famous

4. best—better

6. the worse—the worst

8. more—more than funny ones

10. littler—less

EXERCISE 36.1 Revising sentences with misplaced modifiers

SUGGESTED ANSWERS

2. Singing with verve, the tenor captivated the entire audience.

4. The city spent approximately $12 million on the new stadium.

6. On the day in question, the patient was not able to breathe normally.

8. The clothes that I was giving away were full of holes.

10. A wailing baby with a soggy diaper was quickly kissed by the candidate.

EXERCISE 36.2 Revising squinting modifiers, disruptive modifiers, and split infinitives

SUGGESTED ANSWERS

2. He vividly remembered enjoying the sound of Mrs. McIntosh's singing.

4. The mayor promised that after her reelection she would not raise taxes.

   After her reelection, the mayor promised that she would not raise taxes.

6. The collector who originally owned the painting planned to leave it to a museum.

   The collector who owned the painting planned originally to leave it to a museum.

8. Doctors can now restore limbs that have been partially severed to functioning condition.

Doctors can now restore limbs that have been severed to a partially functioning condition.

10. The speaker said he would answer questions when he finished.

   When he finished, the speaker said he would answer questions.

12. After a long summer under the blazing sun, the compost smelled pretty bad when I turned it.

14. After a long day at work and an evening class, Stella did not want to argue about who was going to do the dishes.

   Stella did not want to argue about who was going to do the dishes after a long day at work and an evening class.

EXERCISE 36.3 Revising dangling modifiers

SUGGESTED ANSWERS

2. When interviewing grieving relatives, reporters show no consideration for their privacy.

4. Chosen for their looks, newscasters often have weak journalistic credentials.

6. Assuming that viewers care about no one except Americans, editorial boards for network news shows reject many international stories.

8. Horrified by stories of bloodshed, most viewers don't recognize the low probability of becoming the victim of crime or terrorism.

10. Not covering less sensational but more common dangers such as reckless driving and diabetes, news broadcasts do not tell viewers what is really likely to hurt them.

EXERCISE 37.1 Revising comma splices and fused sentences

Only one suggested answer is given for each numbered item.

2. The group Human Rights Watch filed a report on Mauritania, a nation in northwest Africa.

4. Members of Mauritania's ruling group are called the Beydanes, an Arab Berber tribe also known as the White Moors.

6. In modern-day Mauritania, many of the Haratin are still slaves; they serve the Beydanes.

8. Mauritania outlawed slavery in 1981, but little has been done to enforce the law.

10. Physical force is not usually used to enslave the Haratin. Rather, they are held by the force of conditioning.

12. By some estimates 300,000 former slaves, who are psychologically and economically dependent, still serve their old masters.

14. In addition, there may be as many as 90,000 Haratin still enslaved; some Beydanes have refused to free their slaves unless the government pays compensation.

16. Of course, slavery must have existed in Mauritania, or there would have been no compelling reason to make a decree to abolish it in 1981.

18. Both the slaveholding Beydanes and the enslaved Haratin are made up largely of Muslims, so some people in Mauritania see resistance to slavery in their country as anti-Muslim.

20. Islamic authorities in Mauritania have agreed that all Muslims are equal; therefore, one Muslim must not enslave another.

EXERCISE 38.1 Eliminating sentence fragments

SUGGESTED ANSWERS

2. September is the perfect time to run outdoors, thus avoiding the wait for a treadmill at a crowded gym.

4. For new college students who live on campus, the Columbus Day weekend often marks the first visit back home. For others, it is Thanksgiving. In any case, the event is often emotionally charged for both parents and students alike.

6. I can't tell if he is skipping the Halloween party because he is genuinely ill, or if he just doesn't have an idea for a costume.

8. My sister and her husband are hosting Thanksgiving dinner at their house this year. With Christmas at my parents' house and New Year's Eve at my cousin's, it should be a busy holiday season!

10. Autumn often begins with hot, summerlike weather. It is often warm enough to go swimming outdoors! And by the end of the season, people are shoveling out their driveways and replacing flip-flops with snow boots.

PUNCTUATION AND MECHANICS

EXERCISE 39.1 Using a comma to set off introductory elements

2. Unlike sterilization, pasteurization does not destroy all the pathogens in a food.

4. While there are many methods of pasteurization, the most commonly used is called HTST (for High Temperature/Short Time).

6. Concerned about the helpful bacteria killed in the pasteurization process, some people recommend drinking raw milk.

8. In stark contrast to their "mainstream" counterparts, cows on raw milk dairy farms are not fed commercial feed.

10. Whatever your opinion on this issue, it is unlikely that the debate will be settled soon.

EXERCISE 39.2   Using a comma in compound sentences

SUGGESTED ANSWERS

2. A biological virus cannot replicate itself, *so* it must inject its DNA into a cell in order to reproduce.

4. These viruses can be totally destructive or basically benign, *yet* when people think of computer viruses, they generally think of the former.

6. Viruses can be distributed through downloads, *or* they can be spread through black-market software.

8. Children love to download computer games from sites they might be unfamiliar with, *so* parents and teachers should teach children about computer security.

10. The world of computer viruses might seem daunting, *but* by following a few basic safety rules, computer users can largely protect themselves.

EXERCISE 39.3   Recognizing restrictive and nonrestrictive elements

2. The clause *who runs in the race* restricts the people who will be receiving T-shirts and backpacks. Therefore, the clause should not take commas.

4. The clause *that have pouches to protect their young* restricts the mammals that are marsupials. Therefore, it should not take commas.

6. The clause *even though it is dishonest and illegal* expresses the idea of contrast. Therefore, it should be set off with commas.

8. The phrase *hit hard during the recent financial crisis* provides extra information about the subject, *The downtown shopping area*. Therefore, it should be set off with commas.

10. The phrase *with anchovies* is essential for the sentence to have any meaning at all. Therefore, the phrase should not take commas.

12. The phrase *red-faced and completely out of breath* provides extra, not essential, information about the boy. It should be set off with commas.

14. The clause *who wishes to complete an independent study* restricts the students who need to find a professor to act as sponsor. Therefore, the clause should not take commas.

EXERCISE 39.4   Using commas to set off items in a series

2. I am looking forward to turning eighteen, being able to vote, and perhaps serving in the military.

4. The moon circles the earth, the earth revolves around the sun, and the sun is just one star among many in the Milky Way galaxy.

6. He is a brilliant, demanding, renowned concert pianist.

8. My top three favorite nineties bands are Pearl Jam, Nirvana, and Soundgarden, in that order.

10. Superficial observation does not provide accurate insight into people's lives — how they feel, what they believe in, how they respond to others.

EXERCISE 39.5   Using commas to set off parenthetical and transitional expressions, contrasting elements, interjections, direct address, and tag questions

2. Doctor Ross, you are over an hour late for our appointment.

4. The West, in fact, has become solidly Republican in presidential elections.

6. Captain Kirk, I'm a doctor, not a madman.

8. One must consider the society as a whole, not just its parts.

10. Mary announced, "Kids, I want you to clean your rooms, not make a bigger mess."

EXERCISE 39.6   Using commas with dates, addresses, titles, numbers, and quotations

2. Correct

4. "Who can match the desperate humorlessness of the adolescent who thinks he is the first to discover seriousness?" asks P. J. Kavanaugh.

6. On July 21, 1969, Neil Armstrong became the first person to walk on he moon.

8. "Neat people are lazier and meaner than sloppy people," according to Suzanne Britt.

10. Correct

EXERCISE 39.7   Eliminating unnecessary commas

2. Insomniacs do indeed wake up at night, but studies have demonstrated that they also have trouble napping during the day.

4. In many cases, insomniacs suffer from anxiety.

6. Correct

8. Sleep therapists recommend going to bed at the same time every night, not watching television in bed, and not reading in bed.

10. While tired people are more dangerous drivers and less productive workers, no one knows for certain if insomnia can actually make them sick.

EXERCISE 40.1   Using semicolons to link clauses

2. The business could no longer afford to pay its bills or its employees; therefore, the owners filed for bankruptcy.

4. Once they live off campus, most students begin cooking their own meals; nevertheless, some choose to maintain their school dining plans.

6. The largest land animal is the African elephant; indeed, typical males reach twenty feet in length and weigh over 16,500 pounds.

8. This expert trail is steep, narrow, and bumpy; only advanced skiers should attempt to go down it.

10. Our senator continues to support tax cuts for the wealthiest Americans; meanwhile, millions remain unemployed.

EXERCISE 40.2   Revising misused semicolons

2. Verbal scores have decreased by more than fifty-four points, while math scores have decreased by more than thirty-six.

4. Finally, I found her at the Humane Society: a beautiful shepherd-collie mix who likes children and plays well with cats.

6. He enjoys commuting to work on the train, although it can get crowded at rush hour.

8. Correct

10. I will meet you at the movies as soon as I finish writing my term paper.

EXERCISE 41.1   Using periods appropriately

2. When her army was defeated by the Romans in 30 BCE and her husband Marc Antony killed himself, some say she committed suicide by means of an asp bite.

4. The empress commissioned the biographies of famous women, decreed that the mourning period for mothers be made equal to that of fathers, and mandated the creation of a character for "human being" that depicted life flowing from a single woman.

6. Ms. Curie discovered two new elements—radium and polonium—and pioneered the understanding of radioactivity.

8. Around 1900, Ms. Addams got herself appointed garbage inspector and rode atop the garbage wagon every morning at 6:00 AM so that she could personally ensure that garbage was being collected in poor districts as well as rich.

10. In 1919, Dr. Hamilton, who lived to be 101 years old, was the first woman ever hired as a professor at Harvard University.

EXERCISE 41.2   Using question marks appropriately

2. "Which Harry Potter book did you like best?" Georgia asked Harriet.

4. "Who wants to go to the pool with me?" asked May.

6. Correct

8. We began to ask what might fix the problem—restarting the computer? closing other programs? using a different browser?

10. I asked her if she would be much longer in the bathroom.

EXERCISE 41.3   Using exclamation points appropriately

Suggested Answers

2. Oh no! We've lost the house!

4. "Go! Go! Go!" roared the crowd as the quarterback sped toward the end zone.

6. It was an ordinary school day, so the child once again came home to an empty house.

8. She exclaimed, "It's too hot!"

10. "This is ridiculous!" sputtered the diner as the waiter brought the wrong order again.

EXERCISE 42.1   Using apostrophes to signal possession

2. Recipients who pass on messages want everyone to hear about a *child's* inspiring fight against cancer or about some dangerous drug, product, or disease.

4. A *hoax's* creators count on *recipients'* kind hearts and concern for the well-being of their families and friends.

6. Have you heard the one about how *deodorants'* ingredients supposedly clog your pores and cause cancer?

8. Some of these scares are probably intended to damage certain *corporations'* reputations by spreading rumors about products.

10. The *Internet's* speed has made such anonymous rumors spread more rapidly than anyone would have thought possible twenty years ago.

EXERCISE 42.2   Using apostrophes to create contractions

2. *You'll* see plenty of advertisements on television for alcoholic beverages, but you *won't* see any for tobacco products.

4. *It's* been almost ten years, but I *can't* forget how I felt on the night we received the terrible news.

6. Restaurants *don't* usually take personal checks, so *I'd* better remember to get some cash before we go.

8. *I'm* always up for a game of chess, but I *wouldn't* want to play for money.

10. Dylan knew she *wouldn't* mind if he *wasn't* able to attend her performance.

EXERCISE 43.1 Using quotation marks to signal direct quotations

2. Correct

4. To paraphrase his words, the planet is in deep trouble if we don't start reducing carbon emissions.

6. Correct

8. "I could not believe the condition of my hometown," he wrote.

10. "Is the computer plugged in?" the technical support operator asked, prompting Harry to snarl, "Yes, I'm not a complete idiot."

EXERCISE 43.2 Using quotation marks for titles and definitions

2. "The Red Wheelbarrow" is often considered to be William Carlos Williams's most important poem.

4. My favorite episode of *Glee* is "Theatricality," especially since the cast performed the Lady Gaga song "Poker Face."

6. After a long hiatus, *Mad Men* returned in March 2012 with a two-hour premiere called "A Little Kiss."

8. At the very end of the last Harry Potter book, in a chapter called "The Prince's Tale," the author finally reveals the true nature of Harry's nemesis, Professor Severus Snape.

10. I realized that all my vocabulary studying had paid off when I saw the word *ephemeral* and knew that it meant "short-lived."

EXERCISE 43.3 Using quotation marks appropriately

SUGGESTED ANSWERS

2. The four-book series that began with the novel *Twilight* by Stephenie Meyer was an enormous success.

4. The soundtrack for the first film in the series includes the hit single "Decode" by the band Paramore.

6. Patty Campbell's editorial review on Amazon.com calls the first novel, *Twilight*, an "exquisite fantasy."

8. The *New York Times* review, by Elizabeth Spires, praises *Twilight*'s ability to depict "a fatal attraction to someone or something dangerously different," but says that the writing is at times "overearnest" and "amateurish."

10. Television shows such as *The Vampire Diaries* have also benefited from a public fascination with the undead.

EXERCISE 44.1 Using parentheses and brackets

2. Are the media really elite, and are they really liberal, as talk-show regulars (Ann Coulter, for example) argue?

4. An article in the *Journal of Communication* discussing the outcome of recent U.S. elections explained that "claiming the media are liberally biased perhaps has become a core rhetorical strategy" used by conservatives (qtd. in Alterman 14).

6. However, liberals are not the only media watchdogs: right-wing organizations, including Accuracy in Media (AIM), also closely examine the way political stories are reported.

8. According to the site's home page, the purpose of Campaign Desk was "to straighten and deepen campaign coverage" as a resource for voters (most of whom rely on media coverage to make decisions about the candidates).

10. And can we forget that as media consumers, we have an obligation to be an informed electorate (even though it's easy to pay attention only to the news that reinforces our own beliefs)?

EXERCISE 44.2   Using dashes

2. Nevertheless, extra charges seem to be added to more and more services all the time.

4. The hidden costs of service fees are irritating—people feel that their bank accounts are being nibbled to death.

6. The "convenience charges" that people have to pay when buying show tickets by telephone are often a substantial percentage of the cost of the ticket.

8. Correct

10. Correct

EXERCISE 44.3   Using colons

2. Ali, Ayaan Hirsi. *Infidel*. New York: Free Press, 2007.

4. The ratio of boys to girls in that preschool is 3:1.

6. Correct

8. Correct

10. My roommate's annoying habits include forgetting to lock the door, leaving dirty dishes in the sink, and playing loud video games late at night.

EXERCISE 44.5   Reviewing punctuation marks

SUGGESTED ANSWERS

2. Some parental efforts do help children; for instance, children whose parents read to them are more likely to enjoy books.

4. A new idea that is popular with many parents of young children is sign language.

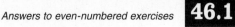

6. By sixteen to eighteen months, most children are able to speak simple words and make themselves understood.

8. Garcia showed that parents could easily teach their children signs for words like *please, more, sleepy,* and *hungry.*

10. Not surprisingly, parents bought the book (and then the video), and now sign-language classes for small children are easy to find.

12. Correct

14. The researchers who developed the study said that the best reason for parents to sign with their children was to allow the children "to communicate what they need and see."

16. Others contend that the children's hand movements stand for concepts, so the movements are sign language.

18. In fact, children who can use sign language are often especially eager to learn how to speak.

20. Any activity that gets parents to spend more time communicating with their children probably has its benefits.

EXERCISE 45.1 Capitalizing

2. The Battle of Lexington and Concord was fought in April 1775.

4. Accepting an award for his score for the film *The High and the Mighty,* Dmitri Tiomkin thanked Beethoven, Brahms, Wagner, and Strauss.

6. We drove east over the Hudson River on the Tappan Zee Bridge.

8. "Bloody Sunday" was a massacre of Catholic protesters in Derry, Northern Ireland, on January 30, 1972.

10. The town in the American South where I was raised had a statue of a Civil War soldier in the center of Main Street.

EXERCISE 46.1 Using abbreviations

2. The power tools, ordinarily used for sanding wood, are placed on a thirty-foot track and plugged in; the sander to reach the end first wins.

4. There are three divisions of belt sander races: the stock division, which races sanders right out of the box; the modified division, which allows any motor the owner wants to add; and the decorative division, which provides a creative outlet for sander owners.

6. The fastest sanders run on very coarse sandpaper—a number sixteen grit is an excellent choice if it's available.

8. The S-B Power Tool Co. in Chicago, maker of Bosch sanders, allows participants to race its tools, but the company does not underwrite races.

10. No one knows what percentage of the nation's power tools have been used for this kind of entertainment.

EXERCISE 46.2 Spelling out numbers and using figures

S<small>UGGESTED</small> A<small>NSWERS</small>

2. After four years of college, I expect to graduate on June 10, 2014.

4. The last time she checked, Kira had 3,457 friends on Facebook; I have only 82, and I like it that way!

6. In the United States, 43 percent of mobile phones in use are smartphones.

8. Correct

10. The bus arrives every weekday at 6:58 AM.

EXERCISE 47.1 Using italics

2. Regional writers produced some American classics, such as Mark Twain's *Huckleberry Finn* and James Fenimore Cooper's *Last of the Mohicans*.

4. Some of the most prolific regional writers were women like Kate Chopin, who wrote her first collection of short stories, *Bayou Folk*, to help support her family.

6. Chopin also departed from regional works to explore women's experiences of marriage, as in her short piece "The Story of an Hour."

8. She later turned these into a novel, *Deephaven*, which she hoped would "teach the world that country people were not . . . ignorant."

10. Many regional stories—Stephen Crane's "The Bride Comes to Yellow Sky" is a prime example—show the writer's concern that an isolated culture is in danger of disappearing.

EXERCISE 48.1 Using hyphens in compounds and with prefixes

2. my ex-mother-in-law

4. devil-may-care attitude

6. Correct

8. pro-NAFTA crowd

10. Correct

EXERCISE 48.2 Using hyphens appropriately

2. The House Un-American Activities Committee was formed in 1937.

4. Remember to drop off your medical forms.

6. Please remind Jane to pick up the clothes from the dry cleaners.

8. I have a nine-year-old daughter, and the younger one is nearly five years old.

10. The sign-up sheet is outside the gymnasium.

FOR MULTILINGUAL WRITERS

EXERCISE 57.1   Expressing subjects and objects explicitly

SUGGESTED ANSWERS

2.   Correct

4.   There are problems with doing everything online, of course.

6.   There are small-time thieves and juvenile pranksters disrupting online services.

8.   A hacker can get enormous amounts of online data, even if they are supposed to be secure.

10.   Internet users must use caution and common sense online, but it is also essential for online information to be safeguarded by security experts.

EXERCISE 57.2   Editing for English word order

SUGGESTED ANSWERS

2.   He displays a flag proudly in the window.
    OR
    He proudly displays a flag in the window.

4.   She should not go into the woods alone.

6.   Sandy drove extremely poorly during her first road test.

8.   Some restaurant guests would like to begin with desserts.

10.   "Speak English fluently," ordered the instructor.

EXERCISE 57.3   Using noun clauses, infinitives, and gerunds appropriately

SUGGESTED ANSWERS

2.   We discussed going to a movie, but we could not agree on what to see.

4.   Correct

6.   Her mother stopped driving on her ninetieth birthday.

8.   Correct

10.   We appreciated getting the invitation.

EXERCISE 57.4   Using adjective clauses appropriately

SUGGESTED ANSWERS

2.   Some students who want to practice speaking more asked us all to help prepare a dinner.

4. A reporter attended the dinner and wrote an article in which he praised the chefs.

6. My mother makes many delicious dishes that come from our homeland.

8. We all come from different places, so those of us who were cooking together had to speak English to communicate.

10. Correct

EXERCISE 57.5 Writing conditional sentences

SUGGESTED ANSWERS

2. If the dot-com boom had continued, that prediction might have come true.

4. If any computer job is announced these days, hundreds of qualified people apply for it.

6. If Indian workers required as much money as Americans do to live, U.S. companies would not be as eager to outsource computer work to the other side of the world.

8. Would fewer Americans be unemployed right now if the dot-com boom had never happened?

10. If American students want to prepare for a secure future, they should consider a specialty like nursing, in which jobs are available and the work cannot be sent abroad.

EXERCISE 58.2 Using determiners appropriately; using articles conventionally

2. Dangerous germs such as salmonella are commonly found in some foods.

4. Many people regularly clean their kitchen counters and cutting boards to remove bacteria.

6. Every time someone wipes a counter with a dirty sponge, more germs are spread around the kitchen.

8. According to research studies, young single men's kitchens tend to have fewer germs than other kitchens.

10. To eliminate many dangerous bacteria from the kitchen, cooks should wash their hands frequently.

EXERCISE 58.4 Positioning modifiers

2. dusty, dry, uninhabited mining town

4. crowded local beach

6. coed volleyball team

8. worthwhile educational program

10. X-rated movie rental

EXERCISE 59.2   Using specified forms of verbs

SUGGESTED ANSWERS

2. The dogs at the kennel barked all night long.
    The dogs at the kennel were barking all night.

4. I brought a present to him on his birthday.
    I am bringing him a present on his birthday.

6. Those teenagers consumed three dozen hamburgers and two cases of pop.
    When I left the picnic, the teenagers were consuming the last of the carrot cake.

8. The pasta steamed in the buffet tray.
    The pasta is steaming up the kitchen.

10. This hamburger tastes good.
    The hamburger had tasted fine until I noticed the fly on the bun.

EXERCISE 59.3   Identifying tenses and forms of verbs

2. was walking: past progressive; struck: simple past
4. has admired: present perfect
6. have attempted: present perfect
8. has driven: present perfect
10. had forgotten: past perfect

EXERCISE 59.4   Using verbs appropriately

2. The Rosetta Stone is *covered* with inscriptions in three ancient languages.

4. At that time, scholars *had been* puzzled by hieroglyphics for centuries.

6. A scholar named Jean François Champollion could *understand* both ancient Greek and modern Egyptian, known as Coptic.

8. From the Coptic inscription, he *learned* to read the hieroglyphics.

10. The hieroglyphics, Demotic, and Greek texts all *contain* a decree from an ancient king.

EXERCISE 60.1   Using prepositions idiomatically

2. into/from/in; during/in
4. up/down/on; on/onto
6. on
8. with
10. to

EXERCISE 60.2 Recognizing and using two-word verbs

2. two-word verb

4. two-word verb

6. verb + preposition

8. two-word verb

10. two-word verb